TERESITA DURKAN

# REFLECTIONS ON A LIFE
*Ó Mhuigheó Go Valparaíso*

**VERITAS**

First published 2005 by
Veritas Publications
7/8 Lower Abbey Street
Dublin 1
Ireland
Email publications@veritas.ie
www.veritas.ie

ISBN 1 85390 981 5

Copyright © Teresita Durkan, 2005

10 9 8 7 6 5 4 3 2 1

A catalogue record for this book
is available from the British Library.


Cover Design by Paula Ryan
Printed in the Republic of Ireland
by Betaprint Dublin

Veritas books are printed on paper made from the wood pulp of
managed forests. For every tree felled, at least one tree is planted,
thereby renewing natural resources.

For Jo Kennedy

# Contents

# Foreword

Reflection is a word with many meanings. For better or worse the reflection that's likely to give most of us pause, from time to time, is our own image in the mirror – which may be about as close as some of us get to being reflective on a daily basis. This is a pity  because it can be rewarding as well as useful to reflect a little on our lives and experiences.

The short autobiographical pieces in this book are an effort to hold a kind of rear-view mirror up to a life, partly so that memories and experiences from the past won't vanish forever into an unreflective waste, but also for the enjoyment, understanding, memories and occasional, worthwhile lessons that the past can still give us.

The Chilean poet Pablo Neruda talks about 'the little things that make life great.' That is, in the main, the chosen territory of these reflections, most of which are brief and written in short-line prose to make them feel even briefer.

*Playa Ancha, Valparaíso*
*June 2005*

A ship from Valparaíso came,
And in the bay her sails were furled.
She brought the wonder of her name,
And tidings from a sunnier world.

'O you must travel far, if you
Would sail away from gloom and wet,
And see beneath the Andes blue,
Our white umbrageous city set'...

Oliver Saint John Gogarty 'The Ship'


*Tháinig long ó Valparaíso.*
*Scaoileadh téad a seol sa chuan.*
*Chuir a h-ainm dom i gcuimhne*
*Ríocht na gréine, tír na mbua.*

*'Gluais,' ar sí 'ar thuras fada*
*liom ó scamall is ó cheo.*
*Tá faoi shleasaibh ghorm Andes*
*Cathair scáthmhar, glé mar sheod'...*

An t-Athair Pádraig de Brún
(A Gaelic translation of Gogarty's 'The Ship')

# Getting to the City of the Ship

The word Valparaíso became familiar to many of us who were schoolchildren in Ireland around the middle of the twentieth century, from a favourite poem in our Irish schoolbooks. This was a Gaelic translation by An tAthair Pádraig de Brún, of 'The Ship' by Oliver Saint John Gogarty, the Dublin man of letters who was a fellow-lodger with James Joyce in Sandycove Tower.

The Gaelic version of the poem turned out to be far more evocative than its English original, possibly because it appealed more directly to the dream of voyaging to faraway places that is latent in the heart of every Celt. So, for many Irish people of that generation, the word Valparaíso came to stand for the goal of an improbable dream-journey.

But most of us in those straitened times had to settle for less exotic destinations. From Louisburgh in west Mayo, I went to Dublin to train as a teacher in Carysfort College where, afterwards, I joined the Sisters of Mercy and was to work for nearly twenty years.

In the 1980s Carysfort was closed as a teacher-training college and I found myself with the freedom and impetus to fulfil an old dream – not of voyaging to Valparaíso, but of going to work in a poor country of the Third World. In 1989 I left Ireland and Mercy community life in Dublin to live and work in South America. My dream was to contribute something to the struggle against poverty on that continent, especially through the education of disadvantaged children.

Choosing Chile was a stroke of good luck, a country so geographically peculiar it barely fits between the Andes and the Pacific, but stretches all the way from the burning Atacama desert to the frozen reaches of the Antarctic. After some uncertain months in Santiago, a chance-opening to do voluntary work in Valparaíso brought me to this old seaport where I found friends and made my home.

Although the word Valparaíso means 'a valley of paradise', nearly half the people of this city are poor, many of them desperately so. But it is a poverty largely of human making. Nature itself is rugged and bountiful here. The coast of central Chile enjoys a mild climate, striking scenery, and proximity to a fertile hinterland which produces fruit, wine and vegetables in abundance while the local fisheries provide a rich variety of sea-foods.

The people are lively and friendly too, and there is still in Valparaíso an old-fashioned sense of community, inclusive enough for even a solitary Irishwoman to find a niche, fit into a family circle, and feel at home. So, did the poem about the ship finally bring me to the City of the Ship? Looking back, I don't really suppose so. This journey began with an appeal by Pope John XXIII which first turned my thoughts to South America and the plight of its oppressed peoples in the early 1960s.

After that, I owe more than I can say or ever repay to the Columban missionaries, men and women, who first welcomed me to Chile for a sabbatical experience in 1984-85, and to the South American Province of the Cross and Passion Sisters who helped me to find a more permanent footing here in 1989. Ongoing is my debt of love and gratitude to Rebecca Perez Roldan and her family for the warmth and support of a Chilean home.

So, when all is said and done, only God knows by what unlikely routes we each find a way to our own City of the Ship.

# The most dramatic and far-reaching change?

According to Eric Hobsbawm, one of the great historians of our time

> the most dramatic and far-reaching change of the second half of the twentieth century, and the one that cuts us off forever from the past, is the death of the peasantry. For since the Neolithic era most human beings had lived off the land and its livestock or harvested the sea as fishers... When the land empties, the cities fill up. The world of the second half of the twentieth century became urbanised as never before.

It was only in the course of compiling these brief autobiographical notes that I began to realise how intimately my own life and that of my family has reflected this deep historical change which Hobsbawm traces across the surface of the globe.

A west of Ireland peasant watching the sun set over the rim of the South Pacific and humming a verse of a Gaelic song composed beside the Atlantic, is certainly not among the first of her kind. It seems a sad thought, though, that she may well be among the last.

# Under the Holy Mountain

I was born in Bunowen
between Croagh Patrick and the Atlantic.
A sandy river-mouth was my first shore.
The searching beam of old Clare Island lighthouse
circled Clew Bay and lit up our back door.
The sound of ocean-surf was my first suantraí,
a long, arrhythmic, lulling, nightly snore.

Faint blue on a rugged horizon,
the straggling mountain-stacks lay back,
steep-banked, from frothing waters.
Each long slow-swelling breaker
seemed to gather and spill a bit of our past.

I was lucky to make it, the ninth of nine,
to be welcomed to life in a place and time
where, as yet, demographics and birth control
hadn't frowned on nine as overload.

Decades later, in a poem by Richard Wilbur,
I'd find a phrase that would evoke strongly for me
the feeling of that rural west of Ireland community
into which I was born in 1937 –
*A small province haunted by the good.*

Wilbur applies that epithet to the earth itself
in a poem whose two final stanzas
sum up, very beautifully, the sense of life
that I was fortunate enough to inherit
in my west Mayo village nearly seven decades ago.

# This is no outer dark

This is no outer dark
But a small province haunted by the good,
Where something may be understood
And where, within the sun's coronal arc,

We keep our proper range,
Aspiring, with this lesser globe of sight,
To gather tokens of the light
Not in the bullion, but in the loose change.

    Richard Wilbur 'Icarium Mare'

As children we were usually very aware of the existence and whereabouts of the loose change in our homes. Some of us kept a hopeful eye out for what might emerge from our mother's purse or our father's pocket. Afterwards, the financial preoccupations of adult life made that kind of small change recede in importance until it came to seem, at times, almost a bit of a bother.

But isn't it true that not all the bullion in Fort Worth could ever bring us as much delight as one of those small hand-warmed coins that we eyed with such longing and spent with so much satisfaction – usually in the nearest sweet-shop – when we were young children?

The loose change of life, the little day-to-day gifts and graces of existence are all around, still, to be enjoyed and appreciated. They can bring us surprise, delight, unexpected chimes and echoes, the pleasures of recognition and memory, and even, on occasion, deep joy, gratitude and wonder. But, like the drops that make up the ocean or the loose change in our pockets, they tend to pass us by unnoticed, much of the time.

'Unless you become as little children you shall not enter the kingdom of heaven.' A practicable and enriching philosophy of life is encapsulated in that slightly-enigmatic gospel saying, a way of seeing and appreciating the world around us, which is close to Richard Wilbur's sense of things. And Wordsworth – using the verb *'watch'* in an old sense – to be alert, wakeful, on the *qui vive* like a sentry – puts the same idea even more directly:

Come forth, and bring with you a heart
That watches and receives.

# De threabh mara mé?

*Nuair a léigh mé 'Na Blátha Craige',*
*dáinín beag ina gceiliúrann Liam Ó Flaitheartaigh*
*an draíocht a imríonn ceol na mara ar na blátha beaga*
*a bhíos ag fás idir aill agus carraig agus cúr na dtonn,*
*b'fhacthas dom gur de'n treabh chéanna mé*
*leis na bláthanna beaga stuacacha sin —*
*nó leis an údar féin, b'fhéidir,*
*ach an t-ádh a bheith liom.*

When I read *Na Blátha Craige*,
a little poem where Liam Ó Flaitheartaigh celebrates
the small hardy rock-flowers called sea-pinks
and the sea-music that holds them bewitched forever
between cliffs and crags and frothing breakers,
I hoped I might turn out to be
made of the same stuff as those stubborn little flowers,
and maybe find some kinship with the author too,
if I were lucky.

# Born into the Europe of the dictators

Hitler, Stalin, Mussolini and Franco –
those were the big names on mainland Europe
when I was born on its western rim in the late 1930s,
and Eamonn de Valera made a strong figure in Ireland.
With eight children already, under the of age sixteen,
my parents must have felt in their hearts
they could do well enough without this extra one.
But I arrived anyway. Easter or spring sap?
April convergence of ripe thrusting energies
generative in salty air and showery seed-time,
of flesh fated to search a far-off shore
for the pith and pitch of its meaning.

My shaping world? A civil war in Spain,
Europe in thrall to murderous dictators,
in Ireland chronic poverty and want,
in England crisis, a royal abdication.
What could I know of Stalin's Gulag hell,
the senseless pain of bomb-fragmented Guernica
or doomed Berlin in ominous Olympiad?

What kin the foetus to its festering times,
spring, summer, winter 1936?

# Getting started

Into that Europe soon to be over-run
by Hitler's jackbooted Nazis and their tanks –
a continent that was again doomed to endure
one of the deadliest wars in human history –
and into a struggling newly-independent Ireland
where money and material comforts were scarce,
I was welcomed by the ordinary love and care
of a big west of Ireland family
earning a bare living from a small farm.

They settled me down without fuss
into my first warm, comfortable spot –
a winter's fireside cradle near a hearth
where turf-ash drifted from the chimney-place
and homespun blankets warmed against cross-draughts.
An ancient cat named Totsy, streaked and greyed,
was sinuous, furry, companionable.

Weaning was slow. The grainy kitchen floor
steadied first steps to gable, garden, meadow.
Geese in damp fields, hens along weedy paths,
the lure of stable, haggard, hedgerow;
turf-stacks beside a winding dusty road,
spring lambs, white moving dots in distant fields,
corncrakes and cuckoos hidden in May grasses
were props for an exploring Mayo childhood,
far from the camps of war and death in Europe.

# Playstations: 1930's style

A leaning gate, a gravelled garden-path,
cornstacks in harvest, harrowed fields in spring,
warm milk from patient, long-tailed, twitching cows,
hayricks in haggards, calves with rippling ribs,
fields where my father swung his frozen arms
against the chill of icy winds in spring,
struggling to tame a cold ungiving soil,
fight thistles, ragwort, rushes, flaggers, whins.
From jutting rocks beside the river-mouth
he forked wet seaweed into dripping creels,
and carted it across a rocky shore
to spread in spring and fertilise small fields.

I climbed the terraced slopes of Fairy Hill,
picked bluebells near its ancient circle-rath
where bonfires had once blazed for exile ships
and weathered boulders sank in the long grass.
In the rabbit-field I used to sit patiently
beside the mouth of a burrow
waiting for a little one to come out and play with me.
But even the smallest ones were too cautious.
Their mothers had probably warned them
that my brothers snared rabbits to sell or eat them.

# Meeting my ancestors 1

*Chreid mé ins na síoga. `Tuige nach gcreidfinn?*
*An charraig mhór liath sin ar Chnoc na Sí,*
*bhí sí mar fholáireamh paiteanta againn.*
*Dá sáithfeá do lámh isteach sa scoilt doimhin*
*a bhí mar bhéal dubh ar éadan na carraige sin*
*d'fhéadfaí tú a shlogadh isteach faoi'n gcré*
*agus ní bhéadh tásc ná tuairisc ort go deo feasta.*
*Bhí scáth orm roimh an duibhe rúnda sin,*
*ríocht mhistéireah na síog,*
*leaba ár sinsir réamh-Chríostaí*
*i ríocht ársa an bháis.*

I believed in the fairies. Why wouldn't I?
We had that big grey boulder on Fairy Hill
as a warning. If you stuck your hand too far
into the slit that ran like a black mouth
across its stony-grey surface,
you could be sucked down into the earth
and disappear forever without leaving a trace.
I felt awe in the presence of that deep darkness,
the mysterious world of the fairies
where our pre-Christian ancestors slept
in an ancient kingdom of the dead.

# Meeting my ancestors 2

*Nuair a ghléasadh mo mháthair muid*
*chun cuairt a thabhairt ar an Tobar Beannaithe,*
*ba mhór an éiri-amach Dómhnaigh againn é.*
*Dhéanaimís an stáisiún timpeall na seanchille,*
*shiúlaimís sa tsruthán, chaithimís tamall beag*
*ag guí ar son na mbeo agus na marbh.*
*Ghlanaimís linn ansin ar lorg cnó nó áirní no sméara dubha,*
*cibé rud so-ite a bhíodh le fáil sa choillín ag bun an chnoic.*
*Mo mháthair ag áirneáin tamall, ag ól té le'na cáirde*
*i dteach beag ceann-tuí ar an gCailleachán.*
*Muidne ag súgradh linn go sásta ar imeall na cille.*

It was always a welcome Sunday outing
when my mother dressed us up
and brought us with her to the Blessed Well.
First we did the station around the old abbey,
then we walked through the stream,
knelt at the well, and prayed for the living and the dead.
After that we made off as fast as we could
to look for hazelnuts, sloes or blackberries,
anything edible we could find
in the little wood at the foot of the hill.
My mother chatted and drank tea with her friends
in a little thatched house in Cailleachán,
while we played away to our heart's content
alongside the graves in the old churchyard.

# Chartless but on course

When I stood on the ancient rath
at the summit of Fairy Hill
and looked out over the Atlantic,
I could see the small dark area
where the Bunowen river
poured its brown waters
into the blue-green reaches of the ocean,
and then I began to sense something
about the shape of my life.

That shifting boundary
between the boggy outflow from the river
and the broad bright sweep of the Atlantic
was clearly visible, but you couldn't chart it –
either beforehand or as you went along
but you could still reach very far places.

.

# No epic life

In the preface to her great novel *Middlemarch*, George Eliot describes Saint Theresa of Avila as 'a woman whose passionate, ideal nature demanded an epic life and found it in the reform of a religious order.' She goes on to reflect:

> That Spanish woman who lived three hundred years ago was certainly not the last of her kind. Many Theresa's have been born who found for themselves no epic life wherein there was a constant unfolding of far-resonant action; perhaps only a life of mistakes, the offspring of a certain spiritual grandeur ill-matched with the meanness of opportunity, perhaps a tragic failure which found no sacred poet and sank unwept into oblivion...
>
> To common eyes, their struggles seemed mere inconsistency and formlessness; for these later-born Theresa's were helped by no coherent social faith and order which could perform the function of knowledge for the ardently willing soul.

In the epilogue to *Middlemarch*, George Eliot reflects on its protagonist, Dorothea Brooke – one of those latter-day unknown Theresa's, whose life was lived not in an age of high ideals or widely-recognised spiritual values like sixteenth-century Spain, but rather among the transitional upheavals, spiritual confusions and social fragmentation that followed the Industrial Revolution in nineteenth-century England. About Dorothea's life, George Eliot concludes:

> Her finely-touched spirit had still its fine issues, though they were not widely visible. Her full nature... spent itself in channels which had no great name on the earth. But the effect of her being on those around her was incalculably diffusive: for the growing good of the world is partly dependent on un-historic acts: and that things are not so ill with you and me as they might have been, is half owing to the number who lived faithfully a hidden life, and rest in unvisited tombs.

A nineteenth-century text with something to offer to people facing the complexities and challenges of the twenty-first century?

# Valparaíso neighbours

I met her on a hot dusty street,
a bouquet of freshly-cut flowers in her arms.
'They're for my mother,' she said,
'It's her anniversary.'
I didn't know her mother,
and I only know her
as one of a little group of neighbours
who regularly supply small needs
and organise treats, gifts and parties
for the poorest among the chronic patients
in our local psychiatric hospital.
Goodness has a feeling, a flavour, a colour,
a lingering unobtrusive fragrance
like a bunch of fresh flowers
lying across a soft arm
on a hot dusty street.

Our young neighbour Gonzalo
is painting windows for his mother these days.
Yesterday he matched his brush-strokes
to the rhythm of some very high-decibel rock music
until someone, not me, complained –
I only wished somebody else would ask him
to mute that ear-shattering beat.
Today he paints to gospel-blues and soul,
each cadence swelling to a deep rich roll.
The woodwork, in both cases, as is right,
turns out a fresh, clean, uniform, matt-white.

# My brother's keeper?

With an improvised handcart, Juanito collects the discards of fruit and vegetables from friendly stall-holders at the street-market. They help to feed his three young children.

He's not a bad fellow, Juanito, neither lazy nor shiftless. He's poor, though, with the most vulnerable poverty of all. He's slow in the head. And in this world where wealth tends to accumulate in the coffers of the already-comfortable, and social justice remains a hope rather than an achieved reality for millions of poor people, Juanito's situation calls for more than passing acts of charity.

It poses a complex political and social challenge for all of us, and demands that we urgently try to change something in our own world – starting, perhaps, with our unexamined sense of total entitlement to excessively-consumerist and wasteful habits of living.

# Valparaíso cats

They do the things all felines do,
bask and yawn, stretch,
and sit about in warm spots,
soak in the sun,
mate and couple and howl at night,
prowl and pounce,
linger over their toilette,
lie across counters,
blink beside fridge-tops,
doze inside sunlit windows.
Only, here they seem
more ubiquitous, more tolerated,
more like sacred cows, somehow,
enjoying immemorial rights and rites –
the prerogatives, let us say,
of an ancient and unmitigated laziness.

Today being wet in Valparaíso
I drank a cup of coffee
in a damp café, emptyish,
with only a white cat for companion,
a beast whose silken hair and warm back
rippled givingly to my touch,
evoking feline caresses, playfulness.
I miss you – that much!

# From the sea

A ship sails into Valparaíso bay, ploughing an ephemeral
furrow across the clean surface of the ocean. No sails, no
masts, no marine graces; just stacks, cranes, containers, a
rusty red hull, a strip of glowing paint above the shifting
water-line, and a rudder that cuts steadily through the deep
cold water. Is she bringing us the spices of the orient? Or
another consignment of cars from Japan?

Why do people – and birds – like so much to stand on the
highest points of rocks by the shore looking out to sea? For
the view? The sense of elevation? The uncluttered airy
space around? The hint of dominance? The achievement of
having got there? To find a good take-off point for a flight
or a dive? Or perhaps the instinctive urge to get a clear
uninterrupted view of where all life on this planet came
from, and where – allowing for an unimaginable variety of
stopovers – it will surely go back to?

Waves?
Curved, crested, slow cartographers
whose enigmatic runes,
deft, cryptic, fleeting hieroglyphs,
seem fingered by the moon
to trace for rinsed oblivion,
earth's endless rippling tunes.

# What it is to grow up

Nectarines and peaches
are called 'baldy' and 'hairy,' respectively
in the blunt argot of our Chilean street-markets.
But the little green peach
that fell on my writing-table today
and showed me the downy-velvet sheen
of her early-spring sheath,
had a youthful grace you wouldn't desecrate
by calling it either of those things.
If she had grown up, though,
she'd probably have come out
on the hairy side.

A youthful eucalyptus,
blue-green creature,
buoyant and round-leaved,
numinous, soft, eager,
longs to grow up.
Her elders, dry and drooping,
parched, sickle-leaved,
untidy, peeling, stooping,
regard her with a certain tenderness,
a disabused nostalgic knowingness.

# Gold at the end of a rainbow

Today in Playa Ancha we were drenched with heavy and unseasonable rain-showers, and then, magically compensated with a spectacular, nearly-perfect rainbow arching all the way across Valparaíso Bay. It had one foot in the distant resort-town of Reñaca, while the other rested lightly on the flank of our hill.

I thought about the pot of gold that, in my childhood, I firmly believed you could find at the end of a rainbow, and called my two small neighbours, Tomás and Vicky, aged five and three respectively, to share this lovely sight, and introduce them to our fine Irish folk-fantasy.

Then, watching them gazing full of excitement at the rainbow's gleaming loveliness, it suddenly dawned on me where you can find the real gold at the end of a rainbow. It's there, surely, in the eyes and hearts – including your own – that can feel delight and a pre-scientific lift of wonder at the sight of the sun painting magical arcs of colour across the sky with tiny droplets of rainwater.

# It can take an earthquake

I saw Valparaíso for the first time in February 1985. I had gone there to make a retreat in the Jesuit Centre because, at forty-eight, I needed to find the courage to make a major change in my life. The retreat coincided, unfortunately, with a series of frightening earth-tremors that became more intense as the days went by until it seemed almost certain that the city was headed for one of its dreaded, full-scale earthquakes.

There's not much you can do in a situation like that except try to stay out in the open as much as possible, so I began to take long walks through the city. One day, after a hot, dusty, hilly climb-and-descent, I sat down to rest in the shadowy interior of an old church. The walls were decorated with murals and canvases depicting the lives of saints who seemed vaguely familiar to me.

After a while I realised I was in the church of the Mercedarian Fathers, a medieval religious community, the first Order of Mercy, which was founded by Peter Nolasco in Barcelona in 1218 to rescue hostages held as captives and slaves by the Moors in North Africa. It was a time when Islamic armies had overrun most of the Iberian peninsula; and taking Christian hostages was a widespread and very lucrative business.

Now, Peter Nolasco and one of his early Catalonian companions – a certain Raymond Nonnatus who gave his life in pledge for the freedom of captives held by the

Algerian Moors, and suffered a very cruel death in captivity – had been recommended to me in my Mercy novitiate long ago, as saints to whom I should try 'to cultivate a special devotion.' But I had never been able to manage it.

They had seemed too distant from me in time and feeling, even though I realised that our Irish Mercy communities (founded by Catherine MacAuley to rescue the poorest Catholics of nineteenth-century Ireland from misery, ignorance, ill-health and squalor) had drawn inspiration from these earlier Mercy saints.

But that day in Valparaíso in 1985, with the earth shaking around me, and hostages once again being held captive by radical Islamic groups in the Lebanon, and my own life no longer anchored as securely as before to some of its earlier certainties, I began to ask myself seriously what a saint is.

Since every human being is, potentially, an expression of God's life, a saint must be someone who expresses that life in some more intense way and shares the energy of that with others so effectively, that – like the stars which still light up the night skies long after they have become physically extinct – the power and vision of a saint's life can go on being a channel of hope, help and inspiration to others, long after the body which housed the original spark has itself turned to dust.

Or, to put it another way, in a world where time is the most elusive, if all-comprehending, of concepts, and also the dimension where our freedom or un-freedom bears in most intimately on each of us, a saint is an ongoing reminder that courage, hope and grace can be stronger than the evil or inertia that is in us and around us, a reminder that we can in fact make the world a better place if only to the power of one, or two, or three...

I did a long meditation that day. But if I had known that forty-eight hours after I left Valparaíso at the end of the retreat, the earthquake would strike and destroy that lovely old Mercedarian church, I might have studied its saints and murals more attentively. By the time I returned to the city in 1989 the church had been demolished to be replaced by a bright collegiate chapel where a single canvas, devotional rather than artistic, depicts the death of Saint Peter Nolasco.

I still meditate from time to time on the life of that Catalonian gentleman who began his career as a soldier but turned away from war to lead a community of men and women who put everything they had – even their lives – on the line to secure the freedom of captives. Commitment of that kind is rare in any age. But in our world where so many people are homeless, nationless, socially-excluded and discriminated against, we can at least make an effort to share space and respect, language, education and citizenship – those ordinary things without which none of us would be free.

# On the shore fish toss...

On the shore fish toss in the stretched nets of Simon,
James and John.
High above, swallows. Wings of butterflies.
Cathedrals.

Czelaw Milosz

There's a cove at the bottom of our hill where fishermen
land their catches in the morning. They haul heavy boats
up a steep gravelly shore and sell the fish there and then to
the highest bidders. Seagulls, pelicans and cats look after
the leftovers.

This kind of fishing, from small open boats, is done
mostly in semi-darkness, in the chill hours between dawn
and breakfast-time. It is hard, cold, body-numbing work.

'Una labor muy sacrificada,' an old man told me.

I didn't ask him who his sacrifices are for. How can any
of us tell that? Or as Robert Frost put it in a different
context, 'Who's to say where the harvest shall stop?'

# Through one window

Small boats, returning from the fishing grounds south and west of the port, speed across my window-space in the mornings, like mobile fly-specks raising tiny trails of turbulence on the grey-blue surface of the ocean. Sitting at my desk, I sometimes think how solid and serviceable their work is – how many good tasty dinners flap and gleam in their scaly holds – by comparison with what I occasionally land.

From my window I can also see headlands, cliffs, sanddunes, a lighthouse, fold upon fold of ochre hills, a bay, an ocean, two cities, roofs, streets, docks, ships, ravines, distant folds of the Andes and, on clear days, Mount Aconcagua – the highest mountain on the western hemisphere.

Behind that my imagination sometimes sketches in the outlines of a more shadowy ancestral landscape, a familiar fretwork from a far-off time and place – the crooked intimate cartography of small fields, furze-ditches and stony hillocks on my father's farm in the west of Ireland, framed against the high rocky cone of Croagh Patrick, Ireland's holy mountain.

# Scáth na Cruaiche

(The shadow of the Reek)

When I climbed Croagh Patrick for the first time, barefoot and fasting, at the age of twelve, I reached the summit in such a wild downpour I thought I'd never get safely home to Bunowen again. Hungry, thirsty, drenched, sore and sorry for myself, I reckoned that this bleak mountain top was one place I'd never want to lay eyes on for the rest of my life.

But the strange pull of those stony heights drew me back. I was to climb it more than twenty times altogether, seven of them in my bare feet. It never got any easier; generally the reverse. The sharp loose shale on the cone near the summit, a steep treacherous scarp just before the top, was always a teeth-gritting endurance-test even when the sun shone brightly over Clew Bay and the view was a reward for all possible pain.

I never knew exactly why I kept climbing it, any more than I could say why I occasionally went back to Saint Patrick's Purgatory on Lough Derg, an even more extended exercise in medieval Celtic penance than toiling up Croagh Patrick in the rain.

'If you can take this, you can take anything.' I never actually said that to myself, but maybe I felt it. Otherwise why face up those jagged slopes, cursing my own foolishness again and again and again?

But if you were born in west Mayo, there was no escaping the holy mountain. Like an ancestral cairn, it was the last familiar shape I saw on the horizon when I left Mayo to join the convent in Dublin in the 1950s. And even now, sixteen years into this different life in Chile, Croagh Patrick is still the silhouette that forms itself, like an insistent shadowy nimbus, whenever I look out my kitchen window on a clear morning after rain to search for the snowy-blue summit of Mount Aconcagua, the highest peak in the Americas.

# The aunts who had to emigrate

This film evoked their exile and their pain,
bewildered hope, life strange and new again
in sweatshop, factory,
streets bright, brash, tough.
To emigrate was life.
Was it enough?

The lively line of starlings on a wire
this vivid sunset, gold-tipped cloudy fire,
*Ragtime* with its plush tin-pan-alley tunes
recalled their life.
What did they win, love, lose?

The roles we play,
the shapes we occupy,
are as ephemeral as a morning sky,
and all our struggles,
all our griefs and pains
fade like a flower
or clouds returned to rain.

# Mixed motives

You could buy cough-no-mores,
bulls-eyes and aniseed balls
in suckable long-lasting quantities
for one brown penny with a hen on it,
in all good Louisburgh sweetshops in the 1940s.
The trouble was pennies were so hard to find.
That's why I liked going to Mass
with my father on Sundays.
He usually managed to locate one for me
in the top, right-hand pocket of his waistcoat.

On the First Friday of the month
when the cows were milked
and the early-morning chores seen to,
my mother dressed in her Sunday best
and went off to Mass in the town.
The visions of a cloistered nun
on the Rue de Bac in Paris,
had produced this welcome little occasion
for country women to meet and chat,
or to shop, consult and drink tea together –
not to mention promises of heavenly rewards –
in the west of Ireland when I was young.

# An old love song

Fear of the different, the disabled, the twitching disfigured boy who was my cousin kept the memory dark and unaccommodated for decades. But the song would float it back to me sometimes, echoingly, hauntingly, insistently, until it became a picture in my mind, lit by the gentling tints of its finally-understood sadness.

A small girl, proud of her new shoes, goes with her mother to visit her aunt who is dying. Her cousin is a disabled boy of twenty who moves his limbs with painful awkwardness. Seeing him fed, adult but inept, frightens her. She's almost afraid to return his friendly smile.

The sisters begin to talk about music, songs they loved, melodies they played, tunes they danced to when they were young. Suddenly the boy begins to sing very clearly and sweetly, 'I wandered today to the hill, Maggie', his mother's name-song, the tune he loves best. His voice is unforgettably true and beautiful.

Now, six decades later, the plaintive melody can still evoke for me the sad beauty hidden in the hollows of an old love song.

# Getting around

Our fastest bicycle was a Coventry Eagle,
a slim semi-racer with scooped-out handlebars,
thin, nippy wheels, and fine, tapering mud-guards.
It was a slender beauty, sturdy and speedy,
energy for errands, velocity for venturing,
halfway between Pegasus and Elijah's chariot.
A gift from our sister Anne in England,
we rode it nonchalantly to the town for messages,
to the bog or the meadow with lunches,
for free-wheeling fun on idle afternoons.
My brother stunt-swerved it at the crossroads
rear-ending on its handlebars with showy machismo.
Sometimes I got tired waiting for my turn
and went off to Derrylahan on the donkey.
Speed wasn't everything.
Alternatives beckoned, even then.
Coventry was fire-bombed.
Hitler burned in his Berlin bunker,
but Churchill left us a small spur of victory
on whirring black wings,
our stylish Mayo wonder-bird,
one exiled Coventry Eagle.

# Humble crafts

One stormy day during the war, a big sea-spar was washed up on the rocks under our land in Derrylahan. My brothers managed to get it ashore after a cold struggle with the waves. It was a thick, fish-smelling, shell-encrusted plank of heavy wood, and it looked very dark and ugly when it came out of the water first. But a few weeks later it appeared in our yard, transformed beyond recognition. Two light, well-made, freshly-painted ladders had emerged – almost miraculously, it seemed to me – from the old water-logged plank.

The skills of blacksmiths, masons and carpenters, working with hard materials like iron, stone and wood, had always fascinated me. I learned a little about crafting softer materials from my mother, when she taught me to tease and card wool which she turned into yarn on her spinning-wheel, and then knitted into winter socks and báinín jerseys for us.

But the change in that old fish-smelling spar fascinated me in some deeper way, maybe because it looked so unpromising to start with. It was to surface in my mind years later when I began to work with words and discovered that – hard or soft, old or new, ugly or beautiful – they generally needed some bit of thought and crafting if they were to earn their keep on a page.

# One bright morning

It was late August, just before going back to school, and the mackerel were shoaling in the bay. My brother and I got up early to go fishing. We had our rods and spinners, bait-sprat and tackle all prepared since the night before.

We started fishing near Keane's bank but we had no luck, not a single bite between us. We moved over to the Kitchen Rocks and tried again, but the mackerel gave us a wide berth there too. Either they had moved far out again or our technique was faulty. We headed for the Nuns' Bathing Place and planned to have our last throw around there beside the big rock called Carraig na Báirneach.

But then, just as we were climbing over the rocks, we hit the jackpot, luck beyond our wildest dreams. In a big rock-pool, left behind after the tide went out, there were dozens of mackerel thrashing around, all trapped together and slapping about trying to escape. They were ours for the taking.

So we filled our bags, nearly afraid to believe we could have struck it so rich. After that we sat down to plan the best way to tell the story of our spectacular catch when we got home. We wanted to make it sound easy and casual, without giving away too much about the precise fishing-skills involved. We couldn't tell a lie though. We knew that. Our mother could smell a lie fifteen miles off, and she had a sally-rod over the fireplace for anyone who forgot the catechism answer: 'No lie can be lawful or innocent, and no motive, however good, can excuse a lie because a lie is always sinful and bad in itself'. The way she said *in itself* was often the prelude to a flexing switch of the sally-rod.

Still, maybe we could just open our bags and let everybody admire those heaps of shining fish and not volunteer any unnecessary details until the first big impact was over anyway. We were sitting there, imagining how we'd handle it, when one of my brother's girlfriends came along the beach. She looked at the fish and cooed with admiration.

It was a bait my fifteen-year-old brother couldn't resist. Joy turned to dejection for me in two minutes. As I moved off along the shore, knowing I wouldn't be missed, the gleam was already fading from my bright morning.

# A valley of paradise

Valparaíso means 'a valley of paradise', an unlikely name for a city that's built on forty-seven hills.

The Spaniards landed here in 1536 but found that Chile offered only very lean pickings after the looted gold of Inca Peru. The Chango people who had fished these isolated coastal waters for centuries knew their home-place as the Valley of Quintil, but, for reasons best known to himself, the Spanish captain, Juan de Saavedra, decided to re-name it Valparaíso.

I arrived here by chance in 1989, having changed continents, hemispheres, oceans, climates and languages, at the age of fifty-two. From the soft lawns and wooded parkland of Carysfort in South Dublin, I found myself in a decrepit old seaport with broken footpaths, decaying houses, rusty funiculars and pot-holed streets. It was a city that, after a brief epoch of prosperity and maritime fame in the nineteenth century, had fallen into slow, sad, and all-too-visible decline, especially when the Panama Canal was opened at the end of the First World War.

So this erstwhile Jewel of the Pacific seemed to have very little to show, on first sight anyway, of the urban lustre that had once made it a celebrated South Pacific seaport. But my notes during the months that followed began to reveal a different, more mixed set of impressions:

In this city parched grass pants for watering
rusty roofs lean into cobbled streets at odd angles,

earthquaked ravines plunge to treacherous depths,
freighters unload along cluttered docks,
and battleships ride at a long grey mole.

Above me a cliff-crevice gleams suddenly
with the shadowy gold of a million thimble-flowers,
litter dances into wind-whirled cornerfuls,
swallows arc to a whitewashed wall,
and a military sentry, rifle at the ready,
confronts three sparrows.

My path follows a snaking bus route,
an ascent of broken steps, cracked paving slabs,
and the weed-grown rails of a creaking funicular.
Around the gleaming crescent of the bay
the city is like a flung horseshoe,
its corkscrew streets and tilting houses
clinging like barnacles to the foothills of the
cordillera.

But at dusk Valparaíso gleams
like a scatter of glinting jewels
thrown carelessly over folds of faded velvet,
when small lights come up on its myriad hills.

As darkness falls, the scalloped outlines
of streetlights, etching pinpoints of brightness
along curving hill-slopes,
seem to flow like streams of stars
down to the black pool of the ocean.

So, was Captain Juan de Saavedra a poet, a prophet, or just
a joker? Who knows? The fact is he left us an evocative name
to keep our dreams alive during the long lean seasons.

# When you are tired or terrified

When you are tired or terrified
your voice slips back into its first old place...

Seamus Heaney

During my first days on the Chilean coast,
I had a strange and oddly-intense experience.
Morning after cool morning
as I stepped from the shower
and towelled the wet gleam from my body,
I was drawn to the fringes of a visual illusion
that repeated itself as insistently
as a sequence in an old dream.


A slanting roof of drab-green metal
in Valparaíso was, suddenly, west Mayo –
the grassy flank of Derrylahan hill
sloping eastwards from the Atlantic
with small fields and stony ditches
tilting crookedly towards Croagh Patrick.


The illusion blotted out every nearer thing –
houses, streets, ships, a harbour, a signal-mast,
ochre hills, two cities, the bay,
the Andes and even the Pacific.

A childhood landscape
etched so deeply in my memory
it pre-empted, for those few seconds,
all the carrying-power of my heart
although I hadn't lived in that countryside
for nearly forty years.

# Falling in love with a tree

Searching for a place to live in Valparaíso in 1989, I climbed a great many hilly streets and walked along any number of crooked cobbled lanes and, without noticing it, I fell in love with a tree – a dusty, thick-leaved, knobby-barked, double-trunked ombú. I didn't know yet it was called an ombú, just as I didn't know the Spanish names for most of the things around me at the time.

Among my most cherished memories of Dublin, the rich verdure and seasonal beauty of the trees in Carysfort Park will always stand out for me: leafy limes, slender birches, ragged old oaks, flowering chestnuts, fine spreading beeches, maples that turned a mellow gold in autumn, and other species that I couldn't tell apart sometimes – like weeping willows and drooping ash.

But in Valparaíso trees were scarce, especially on the hill of Playa Ancha, so I found myself stopping almost instinctively and lingering wistfully under this single dusty ombú that somebody had planted on a curve of Avenida Gran Bretaña, looking down over the docks and out across the bay.

Afterwards, I would come to know a great many beautiful trees in Chile, some in the millennial native forests of the south – and I think that, for once, Pablo Neruda wasn't exaggerating when he said that if you don't know the Chilean rain-forest you have missed one of the great natural riches of the earth.

As time went on I discovered that the ombú, although it can spread its branches alluringly wide, doesn't rate very highly among the trees of Chile. Its soft timber is almost useless, even as firewood. Still, nearly sixteen years later, I seldom pass that curve on Avenida Gran Bretaña without throwing a fond glance in the direction of my old friend the ombú, the leafy companion of a lonely season.

# Above the Andes
## a universe of stars

Last night, sleepless,
I went out to see what the stars were doing.
At three in the morning
they were clustered thickly along the Milky Way,
brilliant diamond-points
piercing the shimmering softness.
Lower down near the horizon,
unfamiliar constellations
made strange glittering shapes
above a dusky rim of the Cordillera.

The orchard pool tried to hold the starlight
but couldn't, anymore than I could conjure sleep.
That sky glowed with intimations of life beyond us,
mysterious and luminous.

I lit no lesser light
but took the stars to bed with me.
They came, eyefuls of them,
to fade on my pillow.

# Pensioned early

I never reflected much on work, the inner quiddity of it. I never had to. In Ireland I usually had too much of it on hand to enjoy the luxury of wondering why I did it. But when I came to Valparaíso first, things were different.

An afternoon siesta was a custom of the country to which I wasn't yet accustomed. So I'd sit under the peach tree after lunch, aware that if I didn't do any work for the rest of the day, nothing much would happen. No sanctions would rebuke my indolence or chart me back to productivity.

So, was it habit, guilt, some old unease, something flickering in the shadow of the peach tree – which was shedding its blossoms just then with a promise of autumn fruitfulness – that sent me doggedly back to the desk each afternoon? I often felt I might just as well have stayed in the garden with the birds and nobody would have been any the poorer.

Gradually, as spring turned to summer, I found myself looking forward to the peace and ease of siesta-time, like all my neighbours. By now I saw it as a welcome space to browse and drowse, a little oasis of restful coolness in the high heat of summer. But even then I'd think sometimes about the peach petals melting in the darkness. 'Work', I'd say to myself, 'the distilled drop has a purity.'

# The scent of eucalyptus

My walk this morning takes me through a sleeping countryside. Wrapped in a misty haze, a fine cooling vapour, the valley of Olmué looks different at dawn. Pines stand darkly green against a close pearly sky. Bleached fields seem almost colourful in their ochre-and-green modulations. Thorn-bushes stand to scattered attention – small, prickly, survivors of a long drought. A single lapwing, perched motionless, surveys a cropped field, and a horse's whinny rises above the other morning sounds – a rooster crowing, dogs barking, small birds chirping and fluttering in the scrub.

In my nostrils, I find the clean scent of eucalyptus – for me one of the most evocative of fragrances, the essence, almost, of this fire-dry landscape. It brings me back to the dusty upland city of Cochabamba in Bolivia where, in the weeks after I first left Ireland, I walked along a muddy canal-bank each morning under a straggle of drooping eucalyptus trees, doggedly trying to hang in somewhere between bleak despair, blind hope, and a too-vivid memory of what I had left behind me.

# To be another's dream

A king is but a foolish laborer
who wastes his blood to be another's dream.

W. B. Yeats


For 'king' read football-idol, rock-star,
fashion-model, film-icon, media-mogul,
sports-prodigy, business-tycoon –
whoever makes it into the most adulatory headlines,
the top media-ratings, the glossiest magazines.

In Valparaíso we're old-fashioned
and have a more inclusive pantheon.
There's a monument here for nearly everybody:
poets, scholars, firemen, fishermen,
sea-captains, explorers, cartographers,
the bald or maybe tonsured friar
who published the country's first newspaper
(some say he has a great deal to answer for),
the frock-coated Victorian who made money
for himself and the city by introducing steam-shipping,
the Lebanese poet who wrote *The Prophet*,
the Chilean, Neruda who composed an ode to fresh air,
to a tomato, to a lemon, to his trousers,
to a chair, a conger eel, the swallows of September...
and won the Nobel Prize.

# TO BE ANOTHER'S DREAM

There's even a hefty statue to the Genoese navigator,
Columbus, who brought in the marauding Spaniards.
As for heroes, liberators, admirals, generals,
presidents, lawyers, mayors and the like,
they have plaques on every street-corner.

I rent a little house here too,
near the Salvation Army.
Like I say, there's a monument
for nearly everybody.

# To the ends of the earth

And you shall be my witnesses
> to the ends of the earth.

Matthew 28

A brace of young Irish women, lay missionaries,
bearers maybe of some ancestral impulse,
trudge through the ochre mud of a Valparaíso hill.
Even the poorest transport doesn't run up there.
Do they dream of green fields and sudden Irish showers
or will they come to love the sultry haze of Pacific
mornings, the orange-and-indigo hues of evening,
the papaya-tinted afterglow of certain winter sunsets?
Why they left Cassiopeia, the Plough, the Pole Star
and the bite and bluster of North Atlantic weathers,
for the mild night skies of central Chile –
where the Southern Cross
flies like a diamond kite
below the Milky Way,
and Orion moves sideways
more like a bright butterfly
than a striding hunter –
is their own secret.

# When Drake was winning seas for England

When Drake was winning seas for England
we sailed in puddles of the past
chasing the ghost of Brendan's mast.

Patrick Kavanagh
'Memory of Brother Michael'

When I read Kavanagh's 'Memory of Brother Michael' in the 1950s, I was young and inclined to think it clever. The Irish Free State into which I was born was too poor to provide a decent living for all its citizens, still less to offer them the hope of a rich and expansive future. So, to find a little dignity for ourselves, we made a virtue of our necessities and tried to compensate for what we lacked, by making capital out of the best of our history.

And so we found ourselves lingering – probably a little naïvely and over-fondly, and certainly a bit too credulously – on the fabled glories of Ireland's Golden Age when the country was said to have been a lighthouse of learning and sanctity for Europe, a veritable Island of Saints and Scholars. In token of which, during most of the twentieth century we sent our emigrants to earn their living in richer countries, and our missionaries to work in poorer, more backward and, on the whole, more climatically-inhospitable places.

So, how far was Patrick Kavanagh justified in making that deprecatory juxtaposition between the peaceful, if fabled, missionary adventuring of Saint Brendan the Navigator in the sixth century, and the piratical voyages of Sir Francis Drake in the sixteenth? The history of Valparaíso throws a chilling light on the subject.

When Drake and his men sailed into the bay here in 1578, they plundered and burned the shipping in the harbour, torched the little settlement with its stores and houses, and slaughtered all the inhabitants who hadn't escaped to the hills. They also set fire to the tiny straw-roofed church, adding insult to injury by ostentatiously quaffing the altar-wine before making off with the sacred vessels.

They continued their career of pillage and murder all the way up the Pacific coast as far as Central America, and the fear they caused everywhere was so great that, for generations afterwards, children in villages along these coasts were called in from play at nightfall with the warning, 'If you stay out after dark El Draque will get you.'

The caption under a line-drawing of Drake in a book about the history of Valparaíso sums up his true historical profile very succinctly: 'A knighted gentleman in England: a murderous pirate in South America.'

About Saint Brendan, a Chilean neighbour recently drew my attention to a newspaper-article crediting him – appreciatively if apocryphally – with having been the first European to make a landfall in any part of the Americas. Unlike subsequent European explorers, the article pointed out, this great Irish navigator and missionary brought no misfortune in his train.

# A South Pacific storm

For fifteen hours it tore around the bay like an enraged animal, attacking hills, ripping the roofs off houses, blowing down walls, tossing ships about as if they were matchwood, lashing the shore-rocks as if it meant to destroy them, and, in an accelerated frenzy of pre-dawn fury, swallowing a steel-hulled cargo-ship with its crew of ten.

Overnight, the Pacific had become a fiendish brown monster. When the wind dropped the bay wore a light vaporous shroud. Hills were wrapped in swathes of mist, and cliffs were scarfed with lengths of floating fog. By nightfall the ocean-surface was like a quilt of black and silver, a patchwork where light and shadow undulated, making strange liquid patterns.

Next morning the sun rose high into rinsed blue skies, the Cordillera stood out sharp and clean on the horizon, Mount Aconcagua showed its snowy peak beyond the border in Argentina. The Pacific stretched away placidly to flat empty horizons and life in the city got back to normal.

All this happened before my eyes. I've felt fear in the presence of this terrifying phenomenon many times now. But I still have no idea where the brown monster comes from or where it goes to. All I know for certain is that it will be back.

# With the poor of the earth

Y con los pobres de la tierra
quiero yo mi suerte echar.
*(And with the poor of the earth,*
*I want to throw in my lot.)*

    José Martí

That Aymara man from Bolivia -
that squat, stooped, determined man
who carried his sick wife to hospital,
a crude seat strapped to his back,
trudging along stony mountain-tracks
winding around a shelved and gaping ravine,
struggling through one sweating day,
one freezing Andean night,
to reach a makeshift clinic –
I have followed him with my uneasy questions.
An ambulance, a roadway, a hospital?
Good treatment for your wife?
Necessary imperatives of civic progress.
But what can progress ever give you
that will not be incomparably less
than what you have,
what you already are,
dwarfing us,
our bought conveniences?

# Ceolta tíre

When my father sang
his songs were in English,
songs of youth and exile,
praises of beautiful women,
stories of love and loss and war.
When his father sang
his songs were often in Gaelic,
songs of drowning and disaster,
ballads about risings and battles,
eulogies to beautiful women,
songs of love and exile and war.
When I sing my songs are in English
or school Irish, or church Latin
or South American Spanish,
and their themes are...nondescript.
Which is why, maybe,
the sound of old instruments
pleases me now:
flute and fiddle,
harp and charango,
bodhrán, bombo, zampoña –
and the thin reed-pipe that came before them all
and will be played by the wind in the hills
long after we're gone.

# Strange echoes

Where the road dwindles to a muddy bridle-path winding among rocks and charred tree-stumps, where a forest fire had spared a few straggling eucalyptus, I found a horseshoe, a clean, almost-unworn horseshoe.

Good luck, I thought, on my first walk through the lovely valley of Olmué. And my thoughts flew halfway round the world to Bunowen where Dolly, our old red mare, died in 1943. When there was no hope for her, they put her down quietly one day before we could race home from school to say another fond, sad, lingering good-bye to her. She's buried on the slope below the old famine-houses...

Suddenly, as if he had come from another world, a stubble-chinned old man, bent and scarce for teeth, appeared out of the trees and stopped me in my tracks. His eye lit straight away on my horseshoe. Two days he was looking for it, he said. So I handed it back. What's luck beside need?

Two brown-and-white lapwings wheeled suddenly into the sky above us. Their shrill cries filled the valley with strange, lingering echoes.

# Crass conjunctions

The biggest aircraft-carrier in the world, the USA warship, the *Ronald Reagan*, is anchored in sight of my kitchen window this morning. Visually, and in every other way that I can think of, it is a floating excrescence, a vast intrusive presence in the peaceful waters of Valparaíso Bay.

On a six-day visit to Chile, it has 6,000 troops on board, navy, air-force and marines. While this swarm of militarised men and women is enjoying shore-leave in Valparaíso today, at least the carrier and its personnel are not, for the time being, engaged in bombing cities, killing people, and destroying lives in Iraq or Afghanistan or elsewhere. But next week, next month, next year – the odds are unfavourable.

So much lethal steel and destructive firepower, such grossly unproductive consumption of fuel and energy in exorbitant quantities, such waste of powerful technology – who needs it in a hungry world? Or on the edge of a country where small children still have to walk ten kilometers to school?

# Nothing is finally true
## which compels us to exclude

Nothing is finally true
      which compels us to exclude.

   Albert Camus

The Mass is the most mysterious though ordinary of all the great rites known to western religious experience. It has added solemnity to the coronation of kings and the obsequies of popes. It has also dignified immeasurably the lives and deaths of countless poor and otherwise uncelebrated people.

I must have attended thousands of Masses in my time, but the one that stands out for me now is a funeral Mass celebrated on a winter's day in the poorest, seediest sector of Valparaíso port – a place where the remains of wrecked lives and lost hopes have been washing up for centuries.

On this occasion it was celebrated for a member of the city's transvestite community – probably the most rejected, cruelly-persecuted, and routinely-despised of all the minority groups who try to find hope and make a life for themselves in this would-be tolerant but sometimes sadly-disrespectful city.

Dee was befriended by an Irish lay missionary who worked in Valparaíso in the 1990s. Born to poverty on one of the city's ragged hills and reared as a boy with a name like Juan or Roberto, in adult life she preferred to be known as Dee, and when she realised that she was going to die young, she asked to be buried in white bridal attire with the full ceremonial of the Catholic Church.

She was lucky that the priest in the port-area was Padre Pepo, a man who knew how it felt to belong to an excluded and penalised minority. During the Pinochet dictatorship, he had to earn his living as an electrician's mate – and realised he was lucky to find any work – because he was ostracised for taking the side of the poor and unjustly-persecuted while that cruel regime held power.

When I remember the moving funeral Mass he celebrated that day for Dee and her family – a genuinely-dignified thanksgiving for a human life – and when I think of the other minorities living in this city and elsewhere who, neither in life nor in death, receive the understanding, respect, or even the simple acceptance of their difference that they merit as human beings, I thank God for people like Padre Pepo and my Irish missionary friend, and I appreciate again the inclusive reach and dignifying power of the Mass.

And when I think of the minorities to which many of us belong, by identity, orientation, race or calling, and which make the challenge to respect, accept, understand and do our best by people of all conditions and categories a more personal and worthwhile experience, I find myself reflecting again on the historic event in which the Mass had its origin.

What is ritually enacted in every Mass is the judicial murder of a good man, one who was mocked, tortured, condemned and crucified as a criminal, rejected by the two most powerful orthodoxies of his time, the political and religious establishments of the holy city of Jerusalem.

When I reflect on this, I wonder why, two thousand

years later, so many people still feel the need to barricade themselves behind the walls of self-righteous and excluding orthodoxies, stigmatising others as outsiders and denying them the right to live peacefully with the personal qualities, gifts and beliefs that God gave them – which is what happened to the Man whose death we commemorate at Mass.

To build a more just and inclusive society – a community where each person can find hope, dignity and respect as well as ordinary recognition and acceptance, without being harshly judged or prejudged or castigated for being different, or despised for not being who they were never born to be, or punished for not believing what they cannot believe – to create such a society remains as urgent a challenge as resisting unjust political systems or oppressive ideologies, and it often requires the same kind of courage.

I think of the great Russian poet, Ana Akhmatova. Armed only with her poetry and her brave, loving heart, she kept faith with the unjustly persecuted and condemned who were swept away into the prison-camps of that most tyrannical of all ideological orthodoxies, Stalin's Soviet Union at the height of its blood-stained power. When others turned their eyes away in fear she stood her ground, suffered and kept faith:

> There I learned how faces fall apart,
> How fear looks out from under the eyelids,
> How deep are the hieroglyphics
> Cut by suffering on people's faces.
> There I learned how silver can inherit
> The black, the ash-blond, overnight,

The smiles that faded from the poor in spirit,
Terror's dry coughing sound.
And I pray not only for myself,
But also for all those who stood there
In the bitter cold, or in the July heat,
Under that red blind prison wall.

Intolerance, persecution and exclusion didn't die with the last dictator or disappear with the advent of a new millennium; they live and thrive inside us and around us. And they can put down insidious roots in our society, sometimes, because they find their seed-ground in our own timorous hearts.

# Desolation

With desolation is the land made desolate
because there is no one that thinketh in his heart.

The Hebrew prophet, Jeremiah.

This evening I had a ringside seat at a Pacific sunset. Glittering expanses of gently-rippling water stretched calmly away to luminous green-and-gold horizons. A twitching touchdown of sanderlings brought feathered life to black rock-tops. Curving breakers held scoops of turquoise in sunlit troughs that swelled into crests and then crumbled to frothy curtains of lacy white as they broke and flowed down along the sides of high jagged rocks.

A line of low-flying pelicans dipped breast-to-breast, almost, with the sunlit ocean as they made their unhurried way southwards. A scene so ordinary, peaceful and beautiful, it soothed my sense of loss, unease and restlessness and cancelled out the edgy energy that's the residue sometimes of broken sleep.

Walking along the beach afterwards over a scalloped stretch of dark-wet sand marked by bird-prints, spindrift and broken seashells, I came face to face with a bleak warning. Two powerful Pacific tides each day are no longer enough to clear away the pollution we now inflict on this lovely coastline. This kind of desolation, the prophet suggests, we can avoid – but only if we learn to 'think in the heart'.

# A ringed plover's nest

We came upon them unexpectedly during a Sunday walk, stumbled over them, trampled on them almost, as we strolled along a familiar seashore. Three tiny speckled eggs nestling unobtrusively – as if they were wearing camouflage – among the flecked pebbles near the mouth of the river. A few rinsed straws, twigs of salty driftwood, a straggle of grass-weed, a wilderness of blue-grey stones, and in the middle of it all, three tiny fragile shells full of warm stirring life, minutely rounded.

No hatching bird in sight, we still felt observed, unwitting intruders, privy to a secret; trying to imagine the ringed neck-feathers, the soft plumage, the white-breasted futures celled in the liquid circuits of those tiny pebble-like eggs.

Afterwards I walked every beach more thoughtfully, at least for a time.

# In a summer meadow

When my father sharpened his scythe to cut the first corner of a new meadow in May, I was always between two minds about the moment. On the one hand, there was that magic fragrance of freshly-cut, clover-rich, wildflower-scented hay spreading its soft perfume through the air, delighting all my senses and assuring me that summer, so long waited for, was here at last.

But on the other hand, there was a job I hated – picking weeds, the scratchy stalks of cow-parsley, rusty-brown docks and prickly thistles that the scythe would leave behind in such long, neat, curving, never-ending rows.

What my seventy-year-old father felt as he faced another season of mowing and haymaking in the small, stony, hillocky meadows of our west-of-Ireland farm, it never occurred to me to ask.

It may have been organic farming, but it was no rustic idyll.

# By the Bunowen River

A memory stays with me from April 2003 when I was with my sister, Evelyn, as she came near the end of her battle with cancer. On a warm day at Easter-time, I thought she was getting better and went to spend a few hours alone at the sea.

So, I'm sitting on a rock near the river and a little boy is throwing stones into the water, again and again and again, delighting in the plop, the splash, the ripple, the achievement. He's about three years old. His parents are walking along the strand on the far side, keeping a watchful eye on him, as I do, because the water is deep and there's a strong current flowing just where the little stone-thrower has positioned himself.

After a while they call him, 'Darcy, we have to go home now.' But Darcy pays no attention. He has lots more stones to throw and the river is flowing along deep and brown. Finally his father comes and forcibly removes him in his arms, and they set off across the strand for the car.

At what looks like a safe distance, his father puts him down to walk for himself, which is Darcy's cue to make another run for the river. He manages to throw several more stones into the water before he's corralled again and finally taken home.

Back in the house Evelyn gets a few more months too. Then September comes and with it her final call. Meanwhile the Bunowen river flows on and on into the great ocean.

# To be and to be just

Maybe we still have time
to be
and to be just.

Pablo Neruda

I didn't enjoy making hay when I was young. It was hard work, and very often there were midges. I hated tying sheaves of oats and barley. The straw scratched my bare arms, and most evenings there were midges. I couldn't stand having to save turf in the bog. I hated the dust, the heat, the backache; and bogs were deadly breeding-grounds for midges. I disliked harvesting carrageen at the shore too. It was cold, wet, slippery work, though the sea wasn't the worst place for midges.

I didn't understand as a child that all those jobs had to be done to feed and educate me and my brothers and sisters, nine of us on a small farm in an impoverished country from which our colonial masters had recently departed leaving the land undeveloped, and the national coffers empty.

I didn't realise back then in the 1930s and '40s that slave-labour – which included child-labour – was being widely used in some of the most technically-advanced countries in the East and West to keep armies equipped and on the move to kill people, destroy their homes, demolish their cities, and ruin their lives.

Now I wonder if I haven't always – even to this day – lived with only the dimmest awareness of what others, men, women and children, have to endure, who share this one world and short life with me, and I know that I have barely begun to appreciate the vastness of my own good fortune.

Sometimes I try to imagine the impossible: a child in Auschwitz who was fortunate enough to have only midges for persecutors? Or an Afghan refugee whose biggest problem is the length of the waiting-list for high-quality medical attention? And then I realise that some part of me is still stuck back there in the egotism of childhood, fretting about midge-bites.

# A población in Santiago

Sunrise,
the Cordillera gleams,
white, misty-blue.
Fissures and angles softly merge
on peaks and slopes.
This day, still new,
will see hunger
sifting with practised hands
through refuse-bins.
In the población
clean morning light
hardens and thins.

Above the receding snows of spring
your kite flies on a delicate string.
Niño, who cares
if the dust of unpaved streets
cakes and hardens on your small feet?
Into clear skies, at finger-flick,
your kite with an invisible twitch
and lofting beauty
soars and swings.

# War is a vast dark jungle

War
is a vast dark jungle.
Peace
begins
in
a single chair.

Pablo Neruda

An American soldier with an unpronounceable Polish
name came from Berlin after the Second World War to
look for his Irish relatives. It turned out that we were
cousins, so I got to show him around, which suited me fine
because he was kindly, friendly and funny, and always
smartly turned-out in one of his GI uniforms. There were
other spin-offs too – coins, candy and chewing-gum.
Showing such a cousin around was a labour of love.

One day I brought him to the church to see a memorial
that had just been unveiled in honour of a Louisburgh
missionary priest, a Columban Father who was killed by
the Japanese troops during their retreat from Manila in
1945.

He turned pale as he read the inscription and then he
said in a strange choking voice, 'I was there, I was in that
god-awful place. The Nips locked those poor bastards into
the church, doused it with kerosene, set it on fire, and then

cleared the hell out of town. We got in too late to save any of them. But, oh my God, that stench from hell… it's in my nostrils still…'

He was still pale and upset as we left the church, and when we got to the gate he did a strange thing. He caught me by the shoulders and spun me around to face him.

'Remember this, little lady,' he said, 'and never forget it even if you live to be a thousand years. War is the real bastard – war is the worst bastard of all.'

# On Robinson Crusoe's island

Señora Eloise told me a story from Isla Juan Fernandez, where the Scottish sailor Alexander Selkirk was marooned in the eighteenth century; Robinson Crusoe's island in the novel by Daniel Defoe. She had worked there as a teacher for seven years.

The story was about five women. Three of them were sisters, and the other two were the daughter and grand-daughter of one of them. These three sisters married men called Recabarren. Their husbands were fishermen, and Recabarren was one of the most common names on the island.

All three husbands lost their lives in drowning disasters, and years later, the daughter – who had also married a Recabarren – was widowed during a South Pacific storm too. Now this woman swore she'd save her daughter from the suffering she and her mother had been through. She forbade the girl to marry, or even to meet, the Recabarren boy who was in love with her. But what islander can outwit fate and the ocean? The girl became pregnant anyway, and the father of her child met his death by drowning too.

'Juan Fernandez is changing,' Eloise told me. 'It has tourists and fishing-exports now along with new technology and rapid communications. But the elements of that old story are still true: the deadly storms that sweep in from the Pacific, the fishermen who put to sea in small boats, and the women who wait for them.'

# Mo thrua amáireach

Mo thrua amáireach gach athair ´s máthair,
    Bean´s páiste atá ag sileadh súl.

    Antoine Ó Raftaire

*Chas mo sheanathair an t-amhrán, Anach Cuain, agus scáth an
bhróin ina shúile. Bhí cuimhne ann fós le'na linn ar chuid acu siúd a
báthadh ag triaill ar aonach na Gaillimhe an lá úd. Ach cailleadh mo
sheanathair sular rugadh mise.*

    *D'fóghlaim mé féin an t-amhrán ar scoil i dTuar Mhic Éide agus
canaim fós é, ó am go chéile, san áit a mbailimíd, los compatriotas
Irlandeses, ag giorrú oíche nó ag cur faid le fiesta. Agus chas mé cupla
véarsa de, aréir, go bog brónach i'm chistin féin nuair a chuala me gur
shlog an tAigéan Ciúin ceathrar iascaire i stoirm gheimhridh amach ó
chósta Valparaíso. Cómharsana dom féin beirt acu, anseo ar Chnoc
Phlaya Ancha.*

My grandfather sang 'Anach Cuain' with sadness in his eyes.
People of his generation still remembered some of those
who had been drowned on that fatal boat-trip to a Galway
fair long ago. But my grandfather died before I was born.

    I learned the song at school in Tourmakeady, and I still
sing it sometimes where we, Irish, gather for an exiles'
celebration or to take part in a Chilean fiesta. And I hummed
a few verses of it last night too, in my own kitchen, as I
thought sadly of the four fishermen who were lost in a
winter storm off the Valparaíso coast. Two of them were
neighbours of my own, here on the hill of Playa Ancha.

# Earthquake

A rifting crunch of fear,
an aftermath of numbness,
long days of cold despair
until the first sound beam is cleared,
a roof-ridge raised,
and the makeshift of tents left
for the raw discomfort of beginnings
or the treachery of cracks and crevices.

Loose rubble is piled high and cleared,
then piled and cleared again in endless increments.
Each replicating tremor of the earth
brings panic no one can control,
a cramping fear around the heart
at another aggression in this saga of constant treacheries.

You can't come to terms with an earthquake.
It's too much like genesis,
that sudden plunge into chaos.
And though it hold the stirrings of new life –
an earth-crust moving towards some new creation
a million millennia from now –
what help is that today?

Better to watch the children playing in the rubble,
babies carried in protective arms,

faces smiling sadly in the metro,
ordinary things that seem more beautiful
and fragile, suddenly,
because now you know
the dark miracle
that brought them to birth.

# Blas sméara dubh'

Blas sméara dubh'
tar éis báistí
ar bharr an tsléibhe.

Brendan Behan 'Uaigneas'

*'Mora con crema'* (blackberry ice-cream)? The girl at the counter gives me a friendly smile. Prune-eyed, she piles a high swirling cone for me with lilac whirls that melt in my mouth like exact memories – of Bunowen where my mother baked blackberry-pies with high crusty roofs and shares for a dozen of us. Her pot-oven sat over the reddened turf-coals, its iron lid glowing brightly first, then cooling to an ashy grey. A thick sweet syrup, a juicy ooze of purpled sugar dripped into the bottom of the oven. We scooped it out with hot spoons and licked our fingers. It tasted like... sloes, crab-apples, hazelnuts, vetches, whatever was free and sweet on the margins of scarcity.

In Carysfort blackberries were barely tolerated. On that well-kept Georgian estate they were the stray bounty of an encroaching briar-patch straggling unappreciated through the damp undergrowth of a lime-and-sycamore grove in a far corner of the park. I picked them during September lunch-breaks, sharing the hour with drowsy birds and alert wasps. My pie-crust was flat and stiff by comparison with my mother's, but its taste brought a touch of the old magic.

In Chile, blackberries ripen in February which is mid-summer, but the sight of a laden bramble can still surprise me at that time of year, like crocuses in a July garden, or daffodils in August. Changing hemispheres is an inconclusive business.

Back in Mayo in the 1990s, I saw blackberries rotting away on the sides of ditches. In Bunowen, the only youngsters picking them were two little German girls on holidays from Frankfurt. They carried the dripping fruit in the thin swags of their sports-socks. We'd have known better than to go home to our mothers with blackberry-juice indelibly staining our good white socks.

# Not what we give
## but what we share...

'A summer Sunday again,
and you'll have visitors,'
the padre said at Mass.
'Friends and relatives on holidays
from Santiago...or the country...or wherever,
dropping in for a chat,
a drink, a bite to eat...'

It reminded me of my mother,
and sister, Evelyn, and living near the sea.

'Well, do your best for them,' he urged.
'Be as hospitable as you can.
Give them a welcome anyway.
It's only once a year...or so...'

They were poor women, his congregation.
They smiled into their laps with wry resignation.
They knew, in a very different way from the padre,
that to celebrate the oldest of human rites –
the breaking of bread –
somebody along the line
has to make a sacrifice.

# A raw truth

My father, working in a windy field along the edge of the Atlantic on a cold spring day in the early 1940s straightened his back from time to time and took shelter under a whin-ditch to smoke his pipe. I sat beside him wrapped in his overcoat and watched the breakers spraying high over the cliffs at the tip of Clare Island.

He pointed, that day, to Carraig na Báirneach, a large bare rock about fifty yards from the shore. Fish, barnacles, winkles, crabs, sand-eels, duileasc, crannach and carrageen, he told me, had eased the hunger of starving people around there during the famines that recurred in west Mayo down to end of the nineteenth century. 'They used to gather a good harvest down there,' he said. My eye followed the stem of his pointing pipe.

Sixty years later, in another country, beside a different ocean, in a new millennium, the scene came vividly back to me. I saw two lean boys gathering shellfish at low tide along a rocky shore near Valparaíso. Rags, wet feet, bent backs, cold and hunger, the chilling hardships of physical poverty – I saw them again through the eyes of my father who was born in 1879 and has been four decades in his grave.

# Old ways passing

*Seanfhear cromtha ag bailiú feamainne dá gharraí fataí,*
*lá bog earraigh ar chladach aimhréidh in Isla Chiloé.*
*Tá a mhac ag obair i bhfeirm bhradán, ag saothrú pá.*
*Agus tá a mhac siúd ag ithe Big Mac nó ag ól Coke*
*ar a bhealach abhaile ó'n gcoláiste i gcathair Castro.*
*Beag an baol go bhfhillfidh seiseann ar sracadh an chladaigh.*

An old man is gathering seaweed for his potato patch
on a soft spring day along a rocky shore in the island of
Chiloé.
His son earns his living working for a salmon-farm,
and that man's son is eating a Big Mac and drinking Coke
on his way home from school in Castro city.
Small chance that young lad will go back
to the hardships of struggling with the sea.

\*\*\*

I know these people from the islands.
I've known them since I was a child.
Darker-skinned, more weather-beaten than us,
smelling of the sea and fish and hardship.
Adept at barter and bargaining
skilful in fireside crafts,
quick to turn a well-spun phrase,
hospitable, lovers of music, dancing,

drinking, verse-making, story-telling.
Will their way of life be lost
in the south of Chile too?
And what is it about mass-culture
that is so fatally seductive?
The lethal allure of comfort,
the slow burn of decay?

# On the Pacific coast

I had such a powerful sense of recognition
when I first stood on the great surfy beach
of Llo Lleo near Puerto San Antonio,
that I felt certain I had been here before.
And who's to say I hadn't?

But, my Mayo version of this liquid immensity
was milder, though still wild to a child's eye.

My God, I've looked for you in worn-out places
where others perhaps had found, or tried to
enshrine you. You are shrineless.

Only the curved light lost in a green wave,
the eye following a seabird's flight,
whorled lines on broken seashells among spindrift –
and the presence or absence
of someone loved and longed for –
locate you near this lunar thunder,
white-crested, sun-shadowed,
where spray spits sand, and surf-lips
suck at the breasts of some endlessness.

How shall I say it?
Lord, I've been alive.
After this there's no death –
that matters.

# 'Where is your God?'

### *Ubi est Deus tuus?*

'Where is your God?'
was a biblical question
our novice mistress was fond of asking
in Carysfort in the 1950s.
I can't remember now what answer
I had back then when I was twenty.
But I was very sure I knew where God was –
the whole blessed trinity –
when I was only seven.

A bearded figure in red and green
in stained glass above the altar-screen
of the parish church; not like us others,
but at least red and green were the Mayo colours.

An infant in a crib at holly-time
with shepherds, ox and ass, a sleeping child,
a blue-cloaked Mary, Joseph, kings with crowns,
a stable like our own, with straw around.

A mysterious figure you couldn't see
though he could see you.
He was watching me,
could read my thoughts,

hear what I said,
knew all I did,
even in bed.

A worthwhile question never ages.
Now, where is your God?

# Saving your soul

The Short Maynooth Catechism was a thin little book with a flimsy paper cover. It was probably the lightest textbook in our 1940s schoolbags, but, definitely the one with the heaviest sanctions.

Saving your soul – or rather the fear of losing it and spending all eternity in the flames of hell – set me thinking about how to find a way out. Birds had no souls to save or lose, I understood. So I used to look speculatively at the ducks. A feathered life, footloose and fancy-free, where all streams led to the river or the sea, might suit me and solve my soul problems.

But then we had to make our First Communion. We learned prayers, hymns and aspirations, reflections, preparations and thanksgivings. We were taught how to stick out our tongues in a modest ladylike way to receive the host, how to walk gracefully in long white dresses, and keep our veils and wreaths from slipping off as we knelt with joined hands, bowed heads, and demurely-lowered eyelids along the altar-rails.

We were allowed to strew flowers in the Corpus Christi procession that year too, kissing each petal as we plucked it from a tiny wicker basket and cast it gracefully over one shoulder towards the monstrance glinting under the gold-fringed canopy where the priest carried the Blessed Sacrament, while we led the way to the town square. We'd get First Communion money too.

The attractions of being a duck faded by comparison. Having a soul had possibilities – even if you had to save it.

# Safe in a dangerous world

During Hitler's war, paraffin for our oil-lamps was scarce, moonless nights in the country were pitch-black, and the Atlantic, a few hundred yards from our backdoor, held mines and other unknown hazards that felt even more fearful when a raft with the legless corpse of a soldier was washed up one morning on a nearby strand.

From the cliffs at the westward tip of Clare Island the lighthouse sent its bright beam across the night waters of the bay, flashing out a warning to ships and seafarers.

But I had my own secret meaning for that bright circling light. Tucked up, safe and warm, in my bed at night and watching it sweep regularly across the wall beside me, I thought it was a guardian-angel with golden wings that God had put there specially to protect me against danger and darkness.

# Nuns

When I was small, nuns were a caste apart, veiled, habited, cloistered and mildly mysterious. We spied on them when they went swimming to see if they were real people.

My first nun taught me to read and write, to handle signs, sums, letters and figures, invaluable skills, tools that would last, though her own life was cut short by a fatal heart disease.

My second nun was thin, pale and delicate. She suffered from cancer and died in her forties but she had a lasting influence on my life. From her, I got my Spanish-sounding name, books that whetted an appetite for reading, a dawning realisation that I was intelligent, hymns with odd rhyming words that I liked, help with a scholarship for secondary school, and the recognition, many years later, that out of her hard life in a cold convent in the west of Ireland during the 1940s, paths to a wider world were opened up for me.

My third nun was a stocky little pile-driver, a small charge of energy and pragmatism on the move under a black veil and habit. But she was clear and methodical and taught us well. From her we learned how to read a newspaper, what concentration camps were, and why we should try to share our pennies, first with the black babies in Africa, and then after the war – but how strange the words sound now – 'with the starving children of Europe'.

# Reluctant choristers

'You don't know what's good for you yet.
You'll only realise it when you get bigger...'
I always begged to differ, inwardly, with my mother
when she came up with that old chestnut.

The elderly nun who gave us music-lessons
must be at least eighty years old,
we – fairly accurately – thought.
But she rapped our knuckles anyway
as hard and often as necessary,
and managed, by push, shove and carrot,
to get us through the first three or four grades
in our piano exams.

I had no gift for any musical instrument,
but more than half-a-century later
I still love the songs, hymns and chants –
especially the fine polyphonic motets –
she taught us, fidgety little conscripts
sent by our mothers to choir-practice,
when we'd much rather be elsewhere.

# Oh Lord, she was Thin

My sister Norah said there was a tombstone
inside the wall of the Protestant church
with the words, 'Oh Lord, she was Thin'
written in big letters on it.
The stone was too narrow, she said,
so they couldn't fit in the last 'e'
when they were carving the inscription
'Oh Lord, she was Thine.'

I didn't believe her
but I could never check it out.
The Protestant church
was strictly out of bounds,
even if we passed it ten times a day.

# Peter the postman

Peter the postman rode the slowest bike in the west. I never saw a mail-delivery more leisurely than his, except in Clare Island once when the mailbag was slung across the back of a visibly-superannuated donkey. The island mailman was getting on in years too. That duo made our Peter look like Speedy Gonzalez.

# An intelligent fish

A farmer by inheritance,
a poacher by conviction,
and a drinking buddy of my father
who was himself no mean poacher,
the best salmon-pool in the river
was only fifty yards from John E's house.
So why should he pay Lord Sligo
for a licence to go fishing?
Anyone could see how the fish jumped up
to greet him as he walked through his own field
along the bank of the river.

His favourite salmon was the one
that spent a whole evening
under a cock of hay in the meadow
reading *The Mayo News*
while the water-bailiff nosed his way
around the territory three times.
Now what would you do
with an intelligent fish like that
but bring him home with you
for a bite of supper?

# Rewards

The lame cobbler in our village gave two of us
a halfpenny to share between us once
when we did messages in the town for him.
It was a lean reward even for those hard times,
but I liked watching him at work,
waxing his long threads, skilful with awl and last,
softening big sheets of leather in a zinc bathtub,
cutting, nicking, measuring, trimming, smoothing,
fitting well-prepared pieces into exact places,
working away with a tapering old knife
that was worn thin from sharpening.
And there he sat in the window-corner,
his crutch propped against the wall,
surrounded by the worn-out shoes he cobbled back to life
to carry us a few more miles along the stony roads
where we couldn't run barefoot in winter –
and where in all his long life,
he had never been able to run at all.

# Shadows

She told us ghost stories in her little kitchen
where the polished range sent out a bright glow
that warmed and lit up the surrounding darkness.
Her eyes had the quick gleam
of a good storyteller too.

But no flame could banish
the shadows in the dark corners.
The shadows remained:
a forced marriage, a violent husband,
fear, pain, secret desperation,
menacing things that we sensed
rather than understood.

Her ghost stories had the ring of truth.

# A famine field

You could still see the ruins of abandoned famine-houses buried under grassy mounds and heaps of scattered stones in the rushy field near the crossroads when I was a child. One of our fields was called Garraí Chaitlín, Kathleen's Garden, but nobody knew anymore what Caitlín's surname had been.

We used to find wild honey there sometimes when my father was mowing the meadow, and a few pale cottage roses still blossomed in June near the hawthorn beside the crossroads.

Otherwise, all traces of Caitlín and her people had vanished, except for that one little field which, for another generation or two, might still raise a passing flicker in someone's mind, by recalling her language and her name.

# A reluctant extra-curricular learner

My mother sent me with a message to the damp house near the river. In a bare comfortless kitchen a woman was sitting at an empty hearth. She got up to welcome me but couldn't straighten her back. She could hardly walk upright anymore.

I stood, wordless and awkward, shifting from one foot to the other. Then I left the package diffidently on the nearest corner of the table and mumbled that I had to go home.

My mother bought flannelette and ran up a layette on her sewing-machine every time a baby was born in that house, swaddling clothes for infants who had nearly as little comfort as the scratchy straw in a manger.

When I carried a can of spring-water home from the well for the tea, the wire handle usually left a painful red ridge across my fingers. So I wasn't very pleased when my mother told me that to carry a can home for the old lady who lived down the road below the brae wasn't just an act of kindness, but a matter of basic good manners.

# Another kind of learning

My father was a man of few words.
Most of what we learned from him,
we had to learn by example.

He wasn't a devout man.
The opposite, in fact.
Listening to him talk,
you'd swear he was a confirmed skeptic.
That's why it impressed me so much
to see him kneeling for a few minutes in the morning,
or lingering on alone after the rosary at night,
taking a quiet time for himself –
for thought, planning, worry, peace, prayer...
Who knows how inner signals are transmitted?

Barley, oats, rye, summer grass
(and a small patch of wheat sometimes
but the land was too poor for it),
spuds, turnips, mangolds, cabbage –
not counting the vegetables my mother
produced in her little kitchen-garden –
those were the crops my father cultivated –
along with us, his nine children.
Not bad, considering he had only thirty acres
of stony land, lashed as often as not
by wild rainstorms blowing in from the Atlantic.

# A thoughtful neighbour

They ostracised her, discreetly but effectively, because she was pregnant before she got married, and both she and they came of highly respectable stock that lived by a sternly self-denying, if judgmental, code.

My mother, a generous-minded woman by nature, wouldn't let me go to the baby's first birthday party. She didn't say why, but I could feel her censure – the closing of ranks around an injured pride of clan.

As time went by the rifts were healed and they all became good friends again, but she had always been a good friend to me. I remember how she took time to calm me down and remove a large paint-stain from my new coat on a day when I was afraid to go home after I incautiously sat eating ice-cream on a newly-painted window-ledge in Long Street. A few days earlier the Archbishop of Tuam had confirmed me as a strong and perfect Christian.

# A hard calling

A hard calling that we took for granted –
so long as it was for somebody else.

He was the brother who bought me my first *new* storybook,
a brightly illustrated copy of *Red Riding Hood* that I could
call my own. Books and clothes were eternally handed
down in our family.

He taught me songs and stories and funny words from
the Gilbert and Sullivan operas he took part in while he
was at boarding school. And when I was a teenager he
taught me how to dance, a slow waltz, a quickstep, a tango
called 'Jealousy'. We'd hum the tunes as we practised the
steps, mamboing around the cement floor of the kitchen.

But then in 1950 he went away to Maynooth and came
back wearing a black suit and a clerical collar. Only
eighteen, and his dancing days were over. Renunciation
was the ground-rule of his calling. He never did a
quickstep around the kitchen again – or anywhere else as
far as I know.

# Goodbye to freedom

When I went away to school at the age of twelve
I had more pounds and ten-shilling notes in my purse
than I ever possessed in my whole life before.
The Louisburgh women to whom I had delivered milk,
didn't allow me to face my exile without some consolation.
The supplies of chocolate and toffee I bought
helped to ease my heartache, a little,
but nothing could ever compensate me
for the sweet taste of my lost freedom.

Behind, lay all the things I loved –
woodbine and meadow-sweet, my mother's flowers,
fuschia and fresia, bumpy boor-tree bark,
bluebells and primroses on Fairy Hill,
fresh swathes of new-mown hay in summer dark,
cobblers and sand-eels, tiny silver fish
that darted like lithe shadows in the sun,
rich reefs of carrageen, rock-pools and sand,
locus of all our barefoot summer fun,
sloes, haws, crab apples, poreens on the ridge,
birds' nests, white roads, brown bogs were left behind
for boarding school, a grey house in a town,
a long hard bench on which I moped and pined.

In the evenings we were allowed out
for supervised walks, filing sedately, two by two,

down the back avenue and out the Balla Road,
neatly turned out in our belted navy coats,
hats, gloves, shiny shoes and long black stockings.

Passing a potato field or a haggard
where men, like my father, were working,
I'd feel like jumping in to give them a hand.
I wanted so much to go back to my old life –
willing even for jobs I had never liked before.

But boarding school was a river of no-return.
There was never any way back to my first freedom.

# A shadow of Anglo-Ireland

Our Claremorris boarding-school was supposed to be haunted by the ghost of an infamous landlord. It had been the home of Denis Brown who was nicknamed Soap-the-Rope for his hangman-like cruelty. This hated High Sheriff of Mayo had hunted rebels with ferocious zeal, and was reputed to have hanged some of them 'with his own hands', off trees on the back avenue of what was now our convent school, in the tragic wake of the 1798 Rising.

I never felt at home in his big grey house, but that was probably not the fault, specifically, of the Honourable Denis Brown who had represented English power and embodied Anglo-Irish greed for my struggling Mayo ancestors who were tenants-at-will on Brown estates during the famine-ridden generations.

But my exile in his drab grey pile lasted only one year anyway, and I shed no tears when I left it for a new Gaelic-speaking college on the shores of Lough Mask.

# A Gaelic schooling

Coláiste Muire in Tourmakeady where I enrolled as a student in 1950 was the creation of our young Irish Free State. Neither the state nor the school was a full generation older than ourselves.

In this preparatory college for teachers, Gaeilge was the language we spoke, and Gaelic the culture we learned to appreciate in a more conscious way. The frothy brown waters of Lough Mask lapped over long scarps of grey-white limestone, and swans with their cygnets nested in the reeds along the edge of the college grounds.

Here, for the first time, I read contemporary poetry, the work of rising young poets of that generation like Máirtín Ó Direáin, Seán Ó Ríordáin, and Máire Mhac an tSaoi. Here, in Liam Ó Flaitheartaigh's *Na Blátha Craige*, I first encountered a congenial image of myself, and here for the first time since I left Bunowen I felt at home and was reasonably content again.

# Things past

What's left now of the lakeside college
where I studied for four years in the 1950s?
An aged building, an orchard gone wild,
a pocked tennis court, a grass-grown pitch;
and, ah yes, a drift of swans and cygnets,
a stand of thinning headland pines,
the softly-lapping waters of Lough Mask,
and the sudden memory of a young man
running across a field in the mornings,
tucking in his shirt-tails as he went,
a lad of our own age, but up before us
to light the furnace and stoke the range
while we got ready for Mass.
That was Jimín.
We said goodbye to him in Dublin in 1954
when he boarded the boat-train for Hollyhead,
and we took a suburban one to Blackrock
to enroll in the old teacher-training college in Carysfort
that saved a handful of us from having to take
the boat to exile, along with him.

# A place called Carysfort

In September 1954 I registered as a student-teacher in Carysfort Training College in Dublin. By then my first life – of childhood and schooling in Mayo – was over though I didn't quite realise it.

Before the year ended I'd have enjoyed my first taste of life in the capital, my first holiday in England, my first sight of the bright lights of London, my first dances in city ballrooms, my first dates with 'real' boyfriends, my first reading of uncensored books, and my first experience of living in the city, away from the rural environment where I had grown up and to which I would not return.

In 1956, when my teacher-training ended, I entered the Sisters of Mercy in Carysfort as a postulant, and, as time went on, this became the place where most of the important issues of my second life were to be decided including, eventually, my decision to leave Ireland for South America.

It seems to me now that the circuitous route which led me to this hill in Valparaíso was implicit in the Mercy journey I began in Carysfort five decades ago. The vow I took there, 'to serve the poor, sick, and ignorant' – a constituency never noticeably present in the elegant if austere environs of Carysfort Park itself, though served with dedication by a great many women who were trained or formed there – would beckon me with growing insistence until I left Ireland for Chile. By then the role that

# A PLACE CALLED CARYSFORT

Carysfort had played in 'the service of the poor sick and ignorant' in Ireland, had finally played itself out.

# What a piece of work

What a piece of work is a man!
How noble in reason! How infinite in faculties!
In form and moving, how express and admirable!
In action how like an angel!
In apprehension how like a god!
The beauty of the world, the paragon of animals!

    Shakespeare: *Hamlet*


To that Renaissance view of humanity,
what image has the twenty-first century
to juxtapose?
A consumer in danger of turning
the world into a wasteland?

# The labouring children

The golf-links lie so near the mill
That almost every day
The laboring children can look out
And see the men at play.

    Sarah Cleghorn (born 1878)

That little verse comes from the Belle Époque, the high era of industrial capitalism and private wealth before the First World War, a time of titanic aspirations to power, profit and luxury, the classical epoch of unbridled expansionism that led to the bloody slaughter of the trenches, the grey nemesis of the Great Depression, and the utter dehumanisation of life itself in Stalin's gulags and Hitler's death-camps.

But such stark contrasts between child-labour and privileged leisure must be out of date now – if only because the labouring children are located at a convenient and disavowing distance from the investor and consumer, never mind the manicured greens of the golfer. Today's labouring children work for their pittance in the backstreets and sweatshops of polluted cities from Mexico to Malaysia, and from Brazil to Bangladesh.

Sadly, September 2003 threw up an even darker image. The *National Geographic* traced the existence of more than twenty million slaves in the world: 'Not people living **like** slaves, working hard for lousy pay,' the magazine insists, but 'about 27 million people, worldwide, who are bought and sold, held captive, brutalised and exploited for profit.'

And with a sense of déjà vu, I read the caption under the photograph of an elderly golfer: 'The slaves in Lake Placid were invisible…People were playing golf at the retirement community, and right behind them was a slave camp.'

This has very little to do with golf, of course, except as an easy image of leisure. But the slaves – and the hundreds of millions of others whose lives are only thinly removed from slavery? Their existence reminds us, if we care to open our eyes, of the unacknowledged cost of our own Belle Époque; and history will hold us responsible for what follows if we make no effort to change things.

# But can we really change things?

On the principle that the longest journey begins with a single step, and that economic and social change has to find its seed-ground in the minds and hearts of human individuals, and express itself concretely in their attitudes and actions, there is something each of us can do.

Consume less thoughtlessly, waste less casually, burn up earth's energy less compulsively, make responsibility – and not the habit of unreflective self-interest – the basis of our investments and transactions... and, in such ways, have some vital energy and resources to spare for projects that offer moral and material support to those who are struggling against poverty, pollution, unfair trade, ignorance, exploitation and deadly diseases.

Resource-sharing is a challenge – both feasible and worthwhile. To be effective it requires focus, effort and persistence. But it is not beyond the reach of anyone. Even an earthworm has a resource to share.

# The litmus test

The curate used a fable
in Olmué church to preach
his text from the prophet Amos,
denouncing the selfish rich.

The cricket chirped all summer
when days were warm and bright.
In winter he went to the well-stocked ant
to ask for something to eat.
'What were you doing in summer?'
inquired the hard-worked ant.
'Singing,' replied the cricket.
Says the ant,
'Push off now and dance.'

'Between those who have gifts
but are selfish,
and the mean whether rich or poor,
there's not much to choose,' says the padre.
'What matters is how you share.'

# Don't count on a clear view

You can't count on having a clear view,
but don't let that be an obstacle.

'What's your dream?' she asked me, my young friend in
Carysfort, more than twenty years ago. But I was in the
office, surrounded by files, reports, timetables, minutes of
meetings, appointments, memos and deferred phone-calls.
I felt middle-aged, hassled, desk-bound, anchored to duty
and responsibility. I was well-intentioned, in a broad way,
but still a talker and a paper-shifter, mostly. I felt blank in
face of the question.

'Dip your bucket where you are.' 'He does much, who
does well, that which he does'. 'Is glas iad na cnoic i bhfhad
uainn.' 'Put your best into the work actually assigned to
you.' Those had been the homely maxims of my
upbringing, so why would I be harbouring dreams?

'Ah, but you must have a dream,' she insisted, so, *noblesse
oblige*, I dredged the depths until I found one that the years
had effectively submerged. 'To go to South America,' I
said, 'to Chile, to throw one small grain into the balance
against poverty, hunger, homelessness, the exploitation
and suffering of children – that Andes-reach of human
misery.'

But at my age, a bookish sort, could I take it? She tossed
her head with youthful nonchalance. So I tested the waters
on a sabbatical leave, and then got my *Nunc dimittis*, quicker

than I expected, when Carysfort was closed and my desk-job disappeared.

Soon after that I left, first for language school in Bolivia, then a poor población in Santiago, and finally this hill in Valparaíso where it's so misty many a morning I can't even see the Andes – though they probably beckoned me down this way in the first instance.

# Puzzling about providence

During my first year in Valparaíso
I used to brood, darkly sometimes, about the way
everything had ended in Carysfort.
One day, Sven, aged five, came to visit me.
First he had ice-cream, then he asked questions.

Lifting the grey feather
that sits like a writer's quill
among my blunt pencils,
he asked, 'Where did you get it?'
'A gift from a seagull,' I told him.
'No,' he shook his head firmly.
'It just fell off his back when he was flying over.'
'Then it's a case for Thornton Wilder,' I murmured.

\*\*\*

Some say we shall never know
and that to the gods we are like the flies
the boys kill on a summer day.
And some say, on the contrary,
that the very sparrows do not lose a feather
that has not been brushed away
by the finger of God.
　　Thornton Wilder

# And that busy office?

Of the thousands of hours I spent there,
so little remains: Rachmaninov, Shostakovitch,
Glen Miller, Abba singing in Spanish...
music played after work of an evening,
memories of a conversation, things read,
sunshine on the moss-green carpet,
crows in the slit of a gabled window,
snow bending the branches of a pine-tree,
some lively presence, or some loved one...

And the work?
Meetings, papers, projects,
boards, buildings, negotiations,
salaries, grants, academic planning,
all vanished now into some deep oblivion.

Is it possible to have forgotten so completely
what once caused me anxiety, frustration,
weariness, hope, anguish, expectation...
and to remember only the small random things
that touched my heart?

And of the hours I spent in that other office,
all I can recall now is sunlight on a vase of daffodils,
an Easter made vivid by crimson tulips,
and a record of old film-themes
stuck in a groove repeating, again and again,
'I was born under a wandering star.'

# In North County Dublin

Lambay, riding green-backed,
yellow-cliffed above a pale blue sea.
A single swift, v-shaped,
skimming low over soft, newly-sprung corn.
In a sunlit field, lone trees, leafless before budding,
sketching traceries across a patched sky,
while a red-roofed house, dark-hedged, cloud-framed,
overlooks a garden noisily visited by crows.
Green fields, regular shapes in infinite tints and contours,
swing fertile acres across sloping hillsides –
organic, old, native to this place.
Myself, a contemplative intruder, celebrant.

Along the strand in Rush one day
I watched the tank-drive of a silken hairy-molly
scaling the pocked side of a drifted sand-bank.
I saw it lift its tiny orange snout, sniff obstacles,
then mobilise its elongated back
and multi-pedal punch, for a steep ascent.
Vaulting the diagonal of a hay-stalk –
show-jumper topping the highest hurdled fence
with practised brush of flicking hoof-tips –
the skill of clearing that slanted straw with myriad toes,
moved me to admiration.

And then with soft-brown rippling body-thrusts
it scaled, nose-sharp, the sand-hill further up

until, thrown back by an invisible gradient,
it toppled, half-defensive, probing for a foothold,
snout twitching, body alert, unbeaten.

It took its bearings, recommenced its climb
holding each tiny gradient with minute persistence
until it reached the haven of a crevice
with deep dark sheltering root-beds.

I sensed its stillness there beyond my sight,
and thought, 'With such small,
powerless, purposed creatures I share the earth.'

# Images of spring in Carysfort

One cool March day I saw,
with the pleasure of an ordinary thing
first attentively observed,
the dual tail-feather panels
of a fast-walking water-hen,
clicking up and down
like synchronated white paddles
describing, in parallel,
a lovely contained see-saw movement
against a neatly up-tailed posterior,
black-feathered.
Words trail behind such tiny perfect things.

With sturdy, waddling gait they passed me by,
paused and detoured, but held a steady course,
a drake and duck on mating business bent,
on finding their accustomed spot, intent.
Fit business for a day in early spring.
Life comes of such small expeditioning.

The beech-tree trunk was sun-warm to my touch.
Its April leaves were soft, its knot-breasts rough.
The lake behind reflected evening light
holding grass-tufts in shadowy silhouette.
I missed old friends who'd walked these paths with me
and picked spring violets underneath this tree.

*Dhá chrann i ngáirdín, ceann geal bán faoi bhláth,*
*'s and dara ceann ar dhath trom iúbhar an bháis.*

Two garden trees, one a bright, white-flowering almond,
and the other a mortally-sombre yew.

# The limits of my language

The limits of my language mean the limits of my world.

Ludwig Wittgenstein

I learned Gaeilge when I went to school. It was new to me then. But I realised afterwards that it was the vernacular of my ancestors and a very ancient Celtic language that had disappeared as the spoken word of my people on the west coast of Mayo only two generations before I was born. By degrees I became proficient enough to use it as my own chosen language, but my parents never understood it. So Gaeilge became my foster-tongue while English, our colonial heritage, remained the language of home life.

In my fifties, I exchanged both of them for a demotic version of Chilean Spanish which has more local peculiarities than the Mayo English of my childhood, and the Gaeilge I spoke in Tourmakeady, and a number of other things put together. Now, to balance my gains with my losses, I write and pray a little in all three languages, but the hymns and chants I like best are in the once-resonant, dimly-understood, semi-defunct Church Latin of my childhood.

The most convincing evidence I have found, though, to support the thesis that the limits of your language mean the limits of your world – or to prove the more hopeful proposition that the frontiers of your language-world can keep expanding even in face of the most adverse odds – has been the surprise of finding that in my Valparaíso neighbourhood, the liveliest use of idiomatic Chilean Spanish – including a rich, curious and vivid vocabulary – belongs to Rebecca Perez Roldan who lost her hearing at the age of eleven.

She hasn't heard a word of any language spoken these last fifty-five years.

# Dreams of a wordless eloquence

When I speak English
I have the urge to explain myself
(which proves, maybe, that English
is not my proper element at all?).
What could be more foolish
than trying to explain yourself?
Does the sea explain itself?
Or a tree? Or the sky?
Or the grass? Or the flowers?
Or the stars?

Better to find a language
in which you can't explain yourself,
aren't even tempted to try.
I thought for a while
I had found such a language
when I first stumbled into Chilean Spanish.
But then it turned out to be like all the rest –
a beguiling will-o'-the wisp force-field
luring you on to try and put words
on the verbally inexpressible.

# Another Ireland

My visitor from Dublin waxed eloquent and indignant, by turns. 'There's any number of Irelands,' he said, 'but the one that's making headlines just now is an aberration, a deviation, a product of mindlessly-imported influences and expensively-borrowed foreign capital...' He paused, waiting for a comment from me. But after sixteen years in Chile, who was I to pass judgment? The Ireland I had known was another country, already part of the past. We did things differently there; often – but not always – for lack of money.

*Eireaball chultúra, óige na gcaogadaí in Éirinn, tógadh muid mar chos-mhuintir i ríocht a cailleadh i bhfhad ó shin i gceo na n-aoiseanna sceite. Bhí muid mar oilithrigh ag díriú bealaigh ar shean-scrínte, tobair bheannaithe, lom-chillíní a coiscreadh fadó le cnámha na naomh agus na n-ollamh.*

*Ach bhí an todchaí ag fás mar gheamhar thart orainn sa phoblacht úr-nua a fógraíodh in ainm na saoirse, agus a thiocfadh i réim go spleodrach le soilse teilifíse agus turais ghealaigh na seascadaí. Lean mé féin de'n tsean-oilithreacht tamall eile nó gur fhógair an chinniúint dom luí na gréine a fhaire ar chósta agus ar chultúr eile.*

*Agus poblacht nua úd na saoirse? Ollmhargadh glórach mearbhallach, ioldaite mar a bhéadh tuar ceatha ann, fásach gliogarnach tarraingteach iasachtach, cuid de'n nua-impireacht cruálach atá ag leathnú a cuid cúmhachta go forleathan anois, agus greim scórnaigh aice ar a cosmhuintir féin in ngach uile tír ó cheann ceann na cruinne?*

We were the rearguard of a culture, the 1950s generation in Ireland. Raised to be foot-soldiers in a kingdom that was vanishing into the mists of an older time, we were like pilgrims making our way to ancient shrines, bare cells consecrated long ago by the bones of saints and scholars.

But the future was springing up around us like new green corn in the young republic that independence had secured for us, a place that would come buoyantly into its own with the television-lights and lunar voyages of the 1960s. I kept to the old pilgrim way for a while longer until it was time for me to watch the sun set on another coast and a different culture.

And that new, free republic? A clamorous, garishly-lit hypermarket, more motley-hued than the rainbow, a vacuous, beguiling, alienating desert, the outpost of a brash new empire which is spreading its sway across the world now as it tightens its grip on the throats of its own hapless foot-soldiers in countries all around the globe?

# Variations on an old theme

An eighteenth-century west-of-Ireland woman called Sarah Parsons comes into my mind sometimes when I see a statue of Chile's Liberator, Bernardo O'Higgins, in the plaza beside the Congress buildings in Valparaíso.

Bernardo's father, Ambrose O'Higgins, was born in County Sligo and rose from emigrant poverty to become Governor of Chile and, eventually, Viceroy for the King of Spain, in Peru. Ballenary, the Irish village of his ancestors, would give its name to the north-Chilean city of Vallenar.

Bernardo was the son Ambrose fathered when he was a provincial governor in his fifties and seduced a Chilean gentlewoman of nineteen with a promise of marriage he would never fulfil – rising colonial officials didn't marry 'native women', however well-born. He made sure the boy was given a good education, but he admitted him to his presence only once, a brief incognito encounter when the lad was about ten years old.

Bernardo grew up to destroy Spanish rule in South America, riding with Generals José San Martín and Simón Bolivar and the armies of the Andes to free his country and transform the history of his continent. He never married, and his descendents, apart from a son called Demetrio who also died unmarried, are not mentioned in the history books.

And Sarah Parsons? She rode south and west through the same countryside that Ambrose O'Higgins left for

Spanish America, and married my great-great-great-grandfather, John William Durkan. They begot a line of west-of-Ireland farmers and have descendents thriving today on four continents.

No bronze statues to any of them, that I know of. Just variations on the theme of Irish emigration – and the realisation that we live in the worlds we create for one another.

# Something you haven't to deserve

'...Home is the place where, when you have to go there,
They have to take you in.'
'I should have called it
Something you somehow haven't to deserve...'

Robert Frost 'The Death of the Hired Man'

Considering that none of us did anything, beforehand, to merit the home or homeland into which we were born, and remembering how our exiles made homes for themselves in countries all over the world for countless generations, how blind and selfish it is of us to stand by, now, complacent and inactive, while doors and national borders are bureaucratically closed against those who still have to travel great distances, in anguish and uncertainty, to find a place to live today, in a century of recurrent and enforced population-displacements.

*An eol duit a Mhuire cá raghair i mbliana*
*ag iarriadh foscaidh do'd leanbh naofa*
*trá a bhfhuil gach doras dúnta ina éadan*
*ag fuath is uabhar an chine daonna?*

*(Do you know, Mary, where you must go this year*
*in search of shelter for your Holy Child,*
*at a time when every door is closed against Him*
*by human hatred and pride?)*

Máirtín Ó Direáin

It may only be bleak honesty for the European Union to exclude Christianity from its proposed constituting texts, if, in an era of unprecedented peace and prosperity, the immigration policies of its member states are moving it further and further away from any possibility of ever realising the most fundamental of all Christian ideals: 'As you would wish that others should do to you, do you also to them, in like manner.'

# Earthed

Measured against an ideal, like perfection,
there's grit and flaw in every human action.

Measured against the dark we stumble in,
one spark of goodness is pure light and gain.

We come from ancient chaos, muddy clay,
and carry the clobber with us all the way.

But, rainbow-like, this flesh and blood and bones,
can catch God's light in strange and subtle tones.

# From the depths

We centre on a life that thirsts for being,
to love and, loving, to be found beloved.
We centre on an inner well, unseen,
strange rippling flows that spring from darker worlds.

We centre on a self to self unknown
except in actions that unveil the thrust
of energy towards animated form,
expressing life in pleasure, pain, love, lust.

We centre on a mystery of moods
unrolling like soft mists on summer nights,
a drift of half-familiar, teasing tunes,
ephemeral glimpses, circling fancy-flights.

But from this formless welter deep within
life finds bright drops, to play and sparkle in.

# About praying

I have often asked myself what is the most essential prayer of all, and now I'm convinced that Saint Paul put his finger on it when he said, 'Teach us to cherish what is of value.'

During the first eight years of my life, more than thirty million people died in battle, were killed in air-raids and naval disasters, were slaughtered in extermination camps, or perished of hunger and exposure or forced labour – because those who wielded power in civilised and technologically-advanced countries, East and West, were unable to recognise what is of value, or lacked the will to respect and cherish it.

But, can we ever really know what is of value? Probably only in the most limited and partial ways. But those limits must surely – always – include the dignity and worth of every individual human life, the will to respect it, and the determination to do our best by it.

For the finer and further enlightenments – especially the lovely gift of cherishing – we can only keep praying and doing our best.

# Gracias!

It seems to me that the world is forever trying to hold a conversation with me. Not just the sun high in the warm blue sky this morning, nor the Pacific Ocean stretching away to silvery-grey horizons, nor the specific hilly headland of Playa Ancha on which I live, nor the haze-softened peaks and folds of the Cordillera, silhouetted against the high white glory of the Andes...

Not just these great natural forces speak to me, nor the stars and dark spaces of the universe at night, nor the awesome piercing brightness of the full moon. Other nearer and more homely things speak to me too; the chair I sit on, the table that supports my elbow and my books; the computer that links me to other minds and worlds; the refrigerator that hums away beside me to keep my food fresh; that food itself which nourishes my body and keeps my mind clear.

And then there's the pen with which I write, and the desk-diary in which I jot down my notes about this would-be conversation with the universe. Now what would such things want to say to me? Well, each has its own agenda. The diary says I came from Dublin, a publisher's gift to remind you that you've been slacking off. The pen says, for all the great capacity of your computer, there are still small jobs that only I can do for you. The sky says, my blue is ephemeral, a set of reflections, illusory but intimately bound up with the freshness of the air you breathe...

The Andes say you've come a long way. The Pacific adds that horizons are not limits...

I look around at the contents of my little kitchen and think I could probably have a conversation with them lasting for the rest of my life without acknowledging even a fraction of what they contribute to my daily wellbeing.

So, maybe it's just as well that my part in this conversation with the universe is very simple – an echo of Shakespeare, in fact: 'I can no other answer make but thanks, and thanks, and ever thanks.' *Infinitas gracias! Míle buíochas!*